THE
PEOPLE FINDER

THE PEOPLE FINDER

Reuniting Relatives,
Finding Friends

A Practical Guide to Finding People
When You've Lost Touch

KAREN BALI

NICHOLAS BREALEY
PUBLISHING

First published by
Nicholas Brealey Publishing in 2007

3–5 Spafield Street   20 Park Plaza, Suite 1115A
Clerkenwell, London   Boston
EC1R 4QB, UK   MA 02116, USA
Tel: +44 (0)20 7239 0360   Tel: (888) BREALEY
Fax: +44 (0)20 7239 0370   Fax: (617) 523 3708
www.nicholasbrealey.com
www.people-search.co.uk

ISBN-13: 978-1-85788-382-4
ISBN-10: 1-85788-382-9

Library of Congress Cataloging-in-Publication Data
Bali, Karen L.
    The people finder : reuniting relatives, finding friends : a practical
guide to finding people when you've lost touch / Karen Bali.
        p. cm.
    Includes bibliographical references and index.
    ISBN-13: 978-1-85788-382-4
    ISBN-10: 1-85788-382-9
    1. Missing persons--Investigation. I. Title.
    HV6762.A3B36 2007
    362.8--dc22

                                                      2006103374

British Library Cataloguing in Publication Data
A catalogue record for this book is available from the
British Library.

Printed in the UK by Clays Ltd, St Ives plc.

CONTENTS

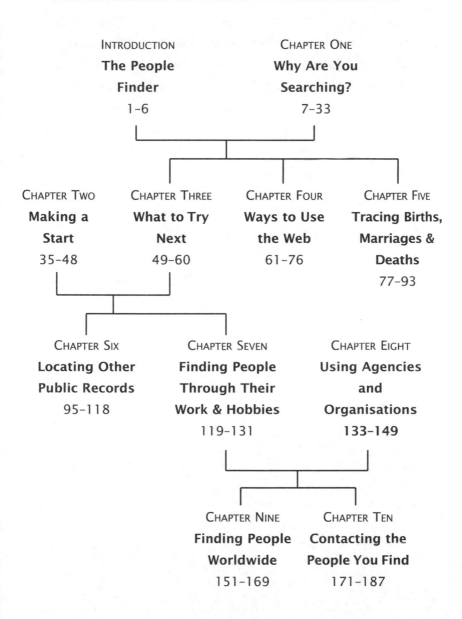

Legal Disclaimer

This book is intended as a guide to help reunite relatives and friends who have lost touch. You should be aware that a 'long-lost' relative or friend may not want to be found, and that persistent approaches that are not welcome may break laws against harassment. The author and publisher accept no responsibility for misuse of the information provided in this book.

Confidentiality

Throughout this book, names and other identifying details have been altered to comply with confidentiality rules and to protect the privacy of clients. Names and details featured in case studies have been changed to protect the identity of the people concerned and their families.

INTRODUCTION

The People Finder is an invaluable resource for anyone who wants to find another person, for whatever reason. It can be used as a do-it-yourself handbook for those who want to attempt a search themselves or as a guide to finding the best possible help.

Based on my work in family research, I have estimated that one in six people would like to find someone for one reason or another, whether it's to meet a practical or emotional need or just out of simple curiosity. If you are looking for an old school friend, a natural parent or an estranged relative, *The People Finder* makes sense of the vast quantities of information you can uncover. It leads you to the most useful contacts and the most valuable resources, and offers nuggets of knowledge to help you locate anyone from your past.

In this book you can find out:

* What to do before you start
* Some simple ideas to try first
* Tips on researching
* Where to find public records
* How to contact specialist organisations
* What to look for on the internet
* How to approach other people for information
* How to plan your reunion
* How to keep in touch

In many cases *The People Finder* will enable you to carry out a search yourself without engaging the services of an investigator or researcher. If you do get stuck, the book offers guidance on obtaining assistance from relevant services and organisations, without spending a fortune.

How People Lose Touch

Losing touch with family members, friends and loved ones is more common today than ever before. A house move, a mislaid address book or a change of phone number can be all it takes. It is not until contact has been lost, however, that you realise the difficulties of locating someone.

Not so long ago, addresses were faithfully recorded, letter writing was common and telephones had not yet taken over. 'Writing and receiving letters was a way of life when I was growing up,' said Mary when she came to me for help. 'My mother would often sit at the dining table writing letters to her sisters, parents and my older brothers. It was my job to run down to the letterbox almost daily. Similarly, we received letters several times a week. The post didn't consist of bank statements and sales literature, like it does now. There was occasionally official correspondence, but mostly it would be letters from family and friends with the latest news, gossip and trivia.' All important news was delivered by post – births, engagements, marriages, deaths – but letters also contained general chitchat like a child getting a first tooth, what happened at the local fair, a romantic scandal. The mundane, such as housework, gardening and the weather, had a place in letters too, and Mary is sure our ancestors felt closer to their relatives through the exchange of handwritten words.

And just a generation or two ago, people did not often leave the area where they were born and remained in close communities throughout their lives. If they did move away, there would almost always be relatives who stayed in the area and contact could be re-established at any time. Today, the average person moves house seven times in their life and the frequency of moves is increasing. It is common for people to live in an area where they have no family connections and for relatives to be scattered across the country. Carl and Joanne are typical.

No ties at all

Carl comes from North London, while Joanne grew up in Somerset. Both went to Sussex to study, which is where they met. By the time Carl left university, a year before Joanne, their relationship was serious and he didn't want to leave her, so he found a job locally. When Joanne graduated, Carl was due for promotion so he remained in the company and Joanne also found work in the area. They had friends, liked the area, bought a house and settled there, seeing their respective families when they could.

After a couple of years they married and started a family. Joanne's parents both died within a year of the birth of the first grandchild and Joanne's brother, her only other close relative, lives in Canada. Carl's parents had divorced and he didn't see his father. When his mother became frail he arranged for her to move to Sussex so that he and

Joanne could be close to her. Carl's two sisters are both married and have moved out of London.

In one generation, due to their random choice of educational establishment, Carl and Joanne have shifted the base of their entire family to a completely new area, and for both of them no ties remain to the place where they grew up.

Another way of keeping in touch is through the telephone. Phone numbers used to remain the same for decades, but now they change frequently too due to house moves, new service operators and altered dialling codes. Mobile phones are replacing landlines as the preferred medium for many people, especially the young, but they are easier to lose, easier to replace, and changing technology means that handsets are updated regularly, often with a different number.

Email addresses are exchanged as much as telephone numbers these days, but they are even more likely to change with jobs and internet service providers.

Easier, faster transportation and more sophisticated telecommunications make distances between cities, countries and continents feel smaller than they really are. A misplaced address or telephone number may not seem important at first. Surely this is the age of information at the touch of a button? Can't we just look someone up?

Unfortunately it's not always that easy: data protection laws mean that everyone has a right to privacy and when you're attempting to find someone you meet many hurdles. Street directories and lists of residents are no longer published, full electoral registers have been withdrawn from public access, more people than ever before (around 70 per cent) choose to have unlisted telephone numbers, and the internet contains many records that are incomplete, out of date or both. That is where this book will help.

Many of the resources described here require access to the internet. Although a high percentage of homes now have computers and an internet connection, not everyone has this facility. If you don't but a friend or relative has the internet at home, you could use their computer or ask them to do some searches for you. Alternatively, public access to the internet is widely available in cafés, libraries, hotels and community centres.

People Search

In my life before family research, I worked in a large public library. One of the most common questions members of the public asked (apart from 'Where are the toilets?') was 'How do I find someone?' This question came up so regularly that I started to gather as much information on the subject as possible and tried to assess the demand. I bought a home computer with Windows 95, shortly followed by one of the first electoral register discs on CD, and started a part-time business, 'People Search'.

At first I advertised in magazines and I was busy from the outset. After two years I felt able to leave my job and build up to a full-time business. I have never been short of work, have completed almost 1,000 searches and usually have an average of 30 cases ongoing at any one time.

I welcome feedback from people who have used my services or followed my advice to locate someone. Please do get in touch if you have had any difficulties, or if you have found someone and would like to share your story – I will be happy to hear from you. My email address is karen@people-search.co.uk.

Chapter One

WHY ARE YOU SEARCHING?

There's always someone who needs to find someone else, for very varied reasons. Here are some of the most common reasons clients have asked me to find people for them.

Family Events

Many people have contacted me for help because they would like someone they've lost touch with to attend a family event, or they want to inform them of important news, such as the death of a family member or the birth of a baby. Often there is a deadline and sometimes this is tight, or occasionally unrealistic ('Find six relatives by Saturday'). While you might have no advance notice of some events, try to allow plenty of time for a search.

If you're planning a **wedding** and preparing the guest list, there are often people you want to invite but you don't know how to contact them. They might be relatives, childhood friends or other people the couple would like to be present.

Similar problems arise with **anniversary** parties, which have become very popular, particularly if they are to celebrate a significant number of years that a couple have been together.

The best man's older brother

Richard wanted to find his best man, Doug Haddon, in order to invite him to a party celebrating his 40th wedding anniversary. He had tried current local and online telephone directories without success. After thinking about Doug for several days, he remembered that Doug had an older brother (possibly called Pete) and that their father had worked at the railway station.

Richard visited the station and spoke with an older member of staff who remembered Doug's father, Jim Haddon. He revealed that Jim had retired about ten years before and moved to a nearby town 'to live with one of his sons'. Richard then went to the main public library for the area. He searched through old editions of phone directories and identified an entry for a 'Mr P Haddon' in the right area.

With the help of library staff, he was able to find the corresponding electoral register entry for the address and locate 'Peter J Haddon, Wendy Haddon and James P Haddon', currently registered at the same address. These details seemed to match Doug's brother and father. Directory enquiries confirmed that the telephone number was unlisted, so Richard decided to write a short note to Peter saying that he was looking for Doug.

Two days later, Peter called and told Richard that Doug was working in Scotland but that he visited his brother and father regularly. Peter contacted Doug, who was very pleased to hear from Richard and delighted to attend the anniversary party. The two are still in touch.

'Decade' birthday celebrations are also growing in popularity. When someone reaches such a milestone and wants to celebrate it, they often feel it's important to reconnect with people from their past.

Funerals are one of the more tricky events in terms of tracing people who should attend, for the simple reason that there is usually no advance warning, leaving little time to locate relatives. If I receive a request for a trace of this nature, particularly if the person sought is a close relative of the deceased, I will often drop everything and pull out all the stops to ensure that the relative is informed in time to pay their last respects.

Family Research

Genealogy is a popular pastime: more people than ever before are interested in the history of their family and have taken steps to discover their ancestors. While most people would think of genealogy in terms of historical research, it is not necessarily merely a search that goes back in time as far as possible. Researchers boast about how far back their family tree extends, as if family lines only go in one direction. Descendant tracing, as opposed to tracing ancestors, attempts to trace forward in time, finding living relatives who are the descendants of a common ancestor. This enables distant relatives to link up and share information.

Last of the line
One fascinating but unfortunately unsuccessful case I worked on was for Mike Pimbury, a man in his mid-70s who

has no children and has never found anyone with the same name as him. Laurie Lee mentions a Mrs Pimbury in his autobiographical novel *Cider with Rosie*, and Mike thinks that is his great-aunt Margaret, but other male relatives have either died childless or had only daughters. Despite tracing the family tree back to 1746 and conducting a worldwide search and a national newspaper appeal, I established that Mike is definitely the final Pimbury in the British Isles and probably the last of the name in the world.

In addition to distant relatives, a large percentage of the population has **living relatives** with whom they have lost touch. This is not uncommon, particularly as the older generation dies off and the next generation moves around. You may remember cousins you knew as children, for example, but with no parents left to ask you've lost the trail. You might wonder what has happened to your relatives and think of them often as you get older, but without the resources to trace them it usually remains something you will do 'one day'.

Tea with cousin Bob

Frank had no family left except the one he had raised. Although he had been happily married for many years, had three children and six grandchildren, he was now a widower with time on his hands. He had been brought up by his father and grandmother – his mother had left when he was a baby – and he had no brothers and sisters. But he did have an uncle with a son called Bob. Frank remembered visiting their house regularly as a child and playing with cousin Bob.

When Bob's parents divorced he went to live with his mother and after their early teenage years Frank and Bob did not see each other again.

Frank asked me to research his family tree, but also asked if I could find his cousin. 'I thought it would be nice,' he said, 'to say hello after all these years.' Bob was eventually located and pleased to hear from Frank. 'I went to tea at Bob's house,' Frank explained, 'and we chatted for hours.' Although due to distance and ill health no more visits have been possible, the two have remained in touch. 'I'm so glad I caught up with old Bob,' said Frank, 'while we both still had the chance.'

Sometimes a person reaches a point in their lives when they just want to know more about their background, perhaps to discover the truth if they realise they have been told lies, or as part of therapy to come to terms with their past.

The other half of history
Tony was in his 50s when his mother passed away. His father had died when he was a baby and little Anthony was adopted by his mother's new husband before he was three years old.

While undergoing counselling for depression following the death of his mother, Tony decided that he needed to know more about his natural father. 'I didn't get along with my stepdad at all,' he explained, 'and I don't think he liked me very much. I have never even seen a photo of my real father and don't know if I have any relatives on that side of my family. I feel as though half of my history is missing and I need to know about my dad so that I can move on and live my life.'

Finding an estranged **father** is the most common request I receive in the course of my work. Your father is obviously one of your closest blood relatives and his genes account for 50 per cent of your biology and personality. Many of my clients feel that part of them is missing if they don't know their father. There is often a need to establish their identity by discovering which physical and emotional traits they have inherited from him. Some clients also feel a sense of abandonment, even anger, and want to confront a father who left them without maintaining contact. Research shows that after relationship breakdown, particularly if the parents were not married, up to 80 per cent of fathers will not be in touch with their child or children after five years.

Just a few decades ago it was shameful to have an illegitimate child and many young couples 'had to get married' if the woman became pregnant. Today things are very different: more than a third of babies born at the beginning of the twenty-first century were not the children of married parents (although a percentage of these were born to couples living together). Illegitimacy in itself does not necessarily mean that close family members lose touch, but it seems to account for a great many of my cases.

A happy reunion

Tom, a sailor from Canada, met British-born Wendy while they were both working in Australia during the late 1960s. They became close friends then began a romantic relationship, despite the fact that Tom was married. They were both young, Wendy explained, and a long way from home. She discovered her pregnancy after Tom had left Australia and she did not expect to see him again.

Wendy returned home to her parents, who supported her, and when her son Darren was just a few months old she married Ron, the only father Darren knew. Ron was a good man and Darren was very fond of him but, after his own marriage and the birth of his first child, Darren felt very strongly that he needed to find out more about his biological father. Knowing that his father was married at the time the baby was conceived and also that Tom knew nothing of his existence was a huge problem to Darren – he did not want to cause upset and disruption. At the same time, his curiosity and burning desire to know his father were becoming overwhelming.

A search was undertaken and discreet enquiries were made, giving no indication of the reason for the search. Tom was eventually traced and an email address obtained from a former colleague. There then began a long process of ensuring that he was the correct person: that he had been in the right part of the world at the time and knew Darren's mother. It was established that his email address was private and that nobody else had access to his personal messages.

After dozens of emails over a few days, without asserting that Tom was the father of Wendy's child, the question came: 'Does this boy think he is my son?' Happily this situation worked out well. Tom had told his wife of his affair with Wendy many years earlier. They had remained together and raised three children. After a positive DNA test (read more about these in Chapter 10), Tom and his wife were happy to welcome Darren as part of the family.

In addition to illegitimacy, a **divorce** in the history of a client's family accounts for a high percentage of my work.

Due to legislation and cost, divorce rates were relatively low until the mid-twentieth century. The number of divorces then rose steadily until the early 1980s and since then has remained between 140,000 and 160,000 a year. More than half of the couples who divorced from 1981 on had at least one child under the age of 16.

Again, searches for estranged fathers are by far the most common. Sometimes the contact was broken by divorce when the client was very young. Often an approach by a child is received well and fathers are delighted to hear from them. Sometimes there is an initial reluctance or hesitation, however, because fathers are not sure how to respond or whether they want to renew contact.

Occasionally fathers are indifferent, even hostile, particularly if they are remarried and have a new family. I have more than once come across fathers who have thought it unnecessary to tell their second (or subsequent) wife that they have already had a family and also withheld from their younger children that they have older half-siblings. Although my initial approach, usually by letter, is discreet and gives no specific information, I have some-times been on the receiving end of a father's anger and indignation at being found if he feels this is a threat to his current way of life.

I have also had a number of cases where fathers are looking for adult children. An acrimonious divorce can lead to a reluctant loss of contact with children because the parents cannot bear to deal with each other. Sometimes the separation was enforced by the mother, often feeling that she was acting in the child's best inter-ests. When this happens some fathers bide their time and wait until their child is an independent adult in the hope that a relationship can then be renewed.

Outcomes in these cases are mixed – sometimes there is a joyful reunion, but sometimes the father's previous absence, often perceived as indifference or abandonment, causes a rift that is too deep to heal and his approach is rejected.

Losing touch with a father has other implications, however. Not only is the child deprived of one relative but of all their **paternal relatives** – one half of their blood family. Grandparents, aunts, uncles and cousins are all important to children growing up, and close relationships can continue throughout life. Someone with a small maternal family, or whose mother is deceased, might find a sense of security in discovering their father's family and forming relationships with them. Even if reconciliation does not work out or the natural father is deceased, it may still be possible to establish a relationship with other rela-tives on that side of the family.

A difficult relationship between any two members of a family can lead to **estrangement** and to a loss of contact with other relatives.

Security in sisterhood

Angela had last seen her older sister Pauline more than 25 years ago. Angela was 11 and her sister 19 when their mother died. Angela had continued to live with her father, but Pauline did not get along with him. Pauline had already left the family home and Angela lost contact with her soon after.

Angela had given little thought to Pauline for a number of years: she was young and had school, friends and her father's relatives to keep her busy. She eventually married and had two daughters who were very close from a young age. When her eldest daughter was 10, Angela's father died suddenly of a heart attack.

It was a few weeks after his funeral that an emotional Angela first contacted me. She had been going through her father's papers and found an old address book containing an entry for Pauline. From then on Angela could not stop thinking about her sister and wanting to contact her. She said, 'I feel as though now my parents are both gone, Pauline is my only link to them and the past. I'm really desperate to find her.'

I was able to trace Pauline, divorced with two teenage sons and living in the next county. Pauline takes up the story.

'When Karen contacted me it was a bit of a surprise. I didn't know that my father had died and frankly wasn't that upset – we had never been very close. Of course I thought about Angela from time to time, but I hadn't imagined her as an adult – she had always been my little kid sister. When I got married and had my sons I used to tell them that they were my family now. I felt secure for the first time in my life.

'When my husband and I broke up I was devastated and became very depressed. I realised that, despite everything, I had married a man just like my father, someone who wanted to control me. My boys keep me going, but they will not be with me for ever. My eldest has a good job and a steady girl-friend, and they're thinking about getting married in a cou-ple of years. My youngest is at college and wants to go to university. I was starting to feel that it would only be a matter of time before I was on my own again.

'Hearing from Angela was the best thing that could have happened. She has been to stay and I have discovered that I am an auntie to her two lovely little girls. My boys are delighted with their new auntie too and love having young cousins to look after. Although I would probably not have thought of trying to find Angela myself, I will be eternally grateful that she decided to find me.'

Adoption

There are an estimated 900,000 adopted people in England and Wales. Formal adoption laws came into force in 1927, and up to the end of 1989 almost 807,000 adop-tions had been recorded. Most adoptions have resulted in complete loss of contact with the birth family.

Finding a famous brother

David Sharp was a wartime baby who was given away on a railway platform after his mother had placed an advert in a newspaper seeking a home for her baby. He was told he was adopted when he was 14, but it was not until he was in his 60s that he tried to trace his natural parents. That was when he discovered he had a younger brother – the novelist Ian McEwan.

David contacted the Salvation Army's Family Tracing Service, who managed to trace two half-siblings, and through them he met his real mother, Rose, who has since died. Rose's sister eventually revealed the full story. When Rose's husband Ernest was away at war she had an affair with another soldier, David McEwan, and became pregnant with David, whom she called Stuart. After Ernest died in the Normandy landings, Rose married David McEwan and had another son, Ian. The two boys grew up no more than a few miles apart, but did not know of each other's existence until 2006. They have very different backgrounds – David became a bricklayer, Ian is an internationally renowned novelist – but they were very pleased to find each other and the families are now in close touch.

information from 'My amazing story, by McEwan's "lost" brother', *Daily Telegraph*, 17 January 17 2007.

Adoption is the one area, more than any other, where it is essential to ensure you have emotional support if you decide to search for your birth relatives; in fact if you were adopted before 1975 at least one counselling interview is compulsory before social services can give you any information from your records. This is important not just at the outset but throughout and after the search.

Try to make it a gradual process over a few months at least, rather than setting out to find a birth relative in the shortest possible time. Once you have found out a little information about your birth mother, for example, it is not unusual to feel an overwhelming need to know as much as possible very quickly. Discovering or being presented with all the facts at once, however, particularly with the possibility of an imminent meeting, can literally be a shock. Adoptees need time to absorb small pieces of information and come to terms with them before moving on to the next stage.

It is best not to attempt this kind of search on your own. If you plan to visit public record sites to look for information about your birth relative, don't go alone – you never know what you may discover. Plans to reunite should be made slowly with the help of a trained intermediary from one of the adoption agencies or the social services department of your local authority. There is usually only one chance to make an approach to your birth family and it is important to get it right.

Local councils throughout the UK have sections and staff that specialise in this area: call the main number for your county, city or municipal authority and ask for post-adoption services. Details of other adoption organisations and charities are listed in Chapter 8.

There are companies and individuals offering adoption search services; you might find them listed in directories or on the internet. However, recent legislation states that only registered Adoption Support Agencies (ASAs) can undertake searching for birth families or adoption intermediary services.

Medical Reasons

Health scares, even ones that result in complete recovery, can also cause people to re-evaluate or seek out medical information from estranged family members.

Coping with cancer

Joanne contacted me after a traumatic year: she had been diagnosed with cancer and undergone a gruelling treatment programme that had left her physically frail and emotionally drained. Her doctors had asked her questions about her family's medical history, many that she could not answer because she had never known her father. She was aware of his name, had an idea of his age and knew the town he had lived in during the late 1960s, when he met her mother.

From this information I was able to trace him and put the two of them in touch. Joanne's father told her that he had suffered the same type of cancer just a few years earlier, and it had been treated successfully. Thankfully Joanne's cancer is now in remission and she is in good health.

An illness that is inherited is not just a predisposition to a particular disorder, such as diabetes or heart disease, but is often due to a **faulty gene** passed on by parents who are sufferers or carriers.

Man on a mission

Bill contacted me to ask for my help in constructing a family tree. This was no ordinary research case, however, as Bill was on a mission. He had inherited a disease that in later life leads to muscular weakness, loss of speech and limited mobility. His brain was unaffected: he was sharp and still able to use a computer to communicate. He just wanted to know how he had inherited this disease.

Apart from being told by the doctors that both his parents must have been carriers, although neither had developed the illness, Bill's only clue was a suspicion that his paternal grandmother may have suffered from the same disease, which was at that time undiagnosed. She had spent a few years in a mental hospital before she died in the 1920s, but this had not really been spoken about within the family.

This was a fascinating case to work on, leading to a great-grandmother from Australia and a great-grandfather from the cotton mills of the north-east of England. I gathered clues from historical records – death certificates and census returns – to build a virtual path that the disease is likely to have taken. Other family lines could then be ruled out, or at least scaled down, as the likely source of the faulty gene.

Research of this nature can often be advantageous to the extended family of a sufferer. Knowing that a faulty gene might be dormant allows relatives the opportunity of being tested to find out if they are **carriers**. The result can then influence a decision to become a parent or enable them to obtain medical screening in the event of a pregnancy.

News that you have a **terminal illness** often brings everything into sharp focus and can be a thunderbolt that precipitates a swift sorting of priorities. Things that would perhaps be done 'some day' move higher up the list when you realise that you have limited time to seek out lost relatives and friends.

In reality, of course, we are all dying. Everyone has limited time to reconcile, reunite or settle scores – it is just a question of degree.

Friends

Childhood friends are sometimes the closest we have and relationships often continue throughout our lives. But people move on, work, marriage and other life events take over, and contact with friends is lost along the way.

Colleagues at work can also become lifelong friends, particularly if the job or career in question involves working closely in cooperation with others. Jobs in a particular industry can attract the same type of people, making it more likely in some cases that you will get along with colleagues better than a random group of people. But it is easy to lose touch when you change jobs.

Armed services personnel often form close and lasting relationships. Living, travelling, working and facing hostility or danger with others often leads to lasting friendships and lifelong bonds. Even after service careers end these people tend to make efforts to stay in touch. Reunions are also more common than in any other career. When contact is lost between service colleagues, however, there are a number of steps that can be taken to help reunite them. See Chapter 4 for websites that can help.

People within other **professions** can also form close and lasting friendships, particularly when they have trained together or shared the same workplace for a number of years. Industry contacts and shared acquaintances can sometimes restore communication quite quickly when former colleagues lose touch, but if one or both leaves the profession it can be much harder to find each other. Chapter 7 contains a number of ideas and resources that might help you locate former colleagues.

Reunions

Reunions in general have become very popular within the last decade. A trend that started in the US with events such as high school reunions has grown and evolved into a whole industry. Armed services reunions have taken place for many years but school, college, family and workplace reunions are also now regular events throughout the UK.

A great deal of credit for this is owed to the phenomenally successful Friends Reunited, a brilliant idea that became a multimillion-pound company in a few short years. Not only did people want to see how their old school friends were doing, they also wanted to meet up. (Read more about Friends Reunited in Chapter 4.)

The psychology behind why people want to reunite with friends from childhood is complicated. Face-value opinions seem to fall into three camps:

* The **enthusiasts** – the ones who have the idea or become active in planning and organising.
* The **attendees** – people who will go along out of curiosity if they don't have to travel too far or if they have nothing else planned.
* The **disinterested** – members of the original group who have no interest in meeting with people from their past.

A number of factors, both obvious and not so obvious, may determine which group you fall into.

If your childhood experiences were happy ones and you have fond memories of school days and friends, you are more likely to want to recreate the thoughts and feelings you had when you were younger.

Age is also a determining factor. For example, if you are in your early 20s with a full life and plans for the future, you may not be interested in remembering a childhood that wasn't so long ago. In mid-life you might feel completely different. A growing realisation of age and mortality can make you long for feelings of a carefree youth.

If your school days were not happy, this can also affect how you feel about reuniting with childhood friends. A young life that was filled with bullying or unhappiness probably isn't something that you want to remember.

Finally, experiences during adulthood and the current state of your life are significant factors in determining your level of interest in a reunion. If life has been good or you view yourself as successful, you are likely to want to share this with school friends – to compare yourself favourably to your peers. If you are less successful or consider yourself a failure, you may not be keen for your former classmates to see you and could worry about feeling inferior if life has not been so good to you.

The class of '76

It took Paul three years to plan his school reunion for the 'Class of '76'. 'I had moved away from the area where I grew up,' he said. 'I took a job 200 miles away, met my wife there and settled happily. We have two lovely teenage children.' Reaching 40 didn't bother Paul at the time, but a couple of years later he registered with Friends Reunited and started exchanging emails with a handful of friends. 'I was in touch with half a dozen people from school and knew about several others who still lived in the area,' he said, 'but our school year consisted of about 150 people. I didn't have a clue what had happened to most of them.'

On a weekend visit to his mother, Paul bumped into another old friend in a pub one evening. They got talking about people they used to know and decided it would be nice to have a reunion sometime. 'Redundancy was the kick-start,' said Paul. 'I suddenly had more time on my hands, no real urgency to get another job for a few months and plenty of time to spend on the internet.' He put the idea of a reunion to 11 of his other school friends, most of whom were enthusiastic. He then picked a date just over a year ahead and started making plans. He tried to form a reunion committee, but this didn't work too well.

'It was funny,' he said, 'once my friends were asked to actually do something, most of them went very quiet! I ended up doing most of the research, planning and organising myself. My friends and I had drawn up a list of people we could remember and I first of all set about locating and contacting as many of them as possible. We contacted 19 people via Friends Reunited and found another 16 just by asking around. Posters in the area of the school and one newspaper advert brought just seven more people. We had around eight months to go and had contacted only a quarter of the potential people from our school year. It was a disappointing time.'

Paul searched the internet, found 192.com (see Chapter 3), took out a subscription and located addresses for another 33 people over the next few weeks. 'At this stage I felt more confident that the reunion would come off,' he said, 'so I booked a venue, paid a deposit and sent out preliminary letters to everyone we had found. Replies came back slowly and many of those contacted had to be chased, but it seemed that almost 60 people were interested and intended to come to the reunion.'

However, other members of the committee became even more apathetic at this stage. 'There was suddenly so much to do and only one other person was really helping me,' explained Paul. 'I arranged the music and catering, had 100 tickets printed, found a supplier for badges, organised a photo board, tried to contact some of our former teachers, then sent out formal requests with reply slips asking for the money – £10 a ticket, which I thought was very reasonable.' He expected a rush of replies with money to reimburse him for expenses so far and to pay for all the necessary supplies and services for the event.

After two weeks only 23 replies had come back. 'At this stage I was really quite angry,' said Paul. 'All that work and people couldn't be bothered just to put a slip in an envelope and send me a tenner. I came close to cancelling the whole thing, feeling very disillusioned. A chat with a relative helped put things into perspective: perhaps some people were on holiday, it was early summer after all, and the letters had been sent out at the beginning of the month. It was possible that some people were waiting for pay day before sending their money.'

Sure enough, a month later Paul had more than 40 replies with payment. The reunion took place very successfully in 2006.

Long-Lost Loves

I occasionally receive enquiries from people who want to trace someone of the opposite sex with whom they formerly had a relationship. This ranges from childhood and teenage sweethearts to former lovers, partners or spouses. Many more men than women apply for this type of search.

Happily single

George called me while he was recovering from heart surgery. He had had a great deal of enforced rest recently and 'too much time to think'. One of the things he had thought about constantly was his divorce from Margaret 25 years previously. 'She was pretty cut up about it,' said George, 'and although the decision was mutual I kept thinking about how distressed she was at the time and how I could have handled things differently.'

George wasn't seeking reconciliation, simply reassurance that Margaret had recovered and moved on. It was so important to him that I agreed to help.

Margaret was located just in time. Her father had died, she was selling his house and was about to move to Edinburgh to set up a dancing school. She was also in the process of changing her name from Margaret to Cecilia, merely because she preferred it. When she called me she was surprised I had contacted her, but pleased to hear that George was still alive and asking after her. She explained that she had changed so much since her marriage broke down and was actually now content to have been single for so long. Since the divorce she had undertaken a programme of self-improvement, which included a complete change of career. She said that she was very happy. Margaret agreed to write to George and for him to have her new address.

George's mind was at rest after he received the letter. 'We are going to exchange Christmas cards and news every year,' he told me, 'which suits me just fine. I guess I'll have to find something else to worry about now!'

If your search is for a lost love, old sweetheart or former partner, this is the stage at which to consider very carefully your reasons and expectations. People rarely think about significant others in their lives unless they hold some hope of reconciliation. But although magazines and newspapers sometimes carry stories of long-lost loves meeting up after many years then getting married, this 'happy ever after' has never been the outcome of any search of this nature I have been involved with.

In the majority of the 100 or so cases I have taken on where a client has requested a search for a former girl-friend, boyfriend or spouse, when the person was found contact was not welcome and the client was left disap-pointed. Occasionally there has been an exchange of let-ters, a phone call or two and perhaps even a meeting to catch up with news. Some former sweethearts have remained friends and kept in touch. Nevertheless, however fond your memories of a special person from the past, it is likely that they now have a happy life with another partner. By all means try to find them if it is important to you, but do so with your feet firmly on the ground.

Legal Reasons

I spend a high percentage of my time these days carrying out work for solicitors and executors, seeking beneficiar-ies of **wills**. Sometimes a will is made years, even decades, before the person dies. In that time the beneficiaries may have moved, changed name, left the country or died. Locating the right people to inform them of the death and their inheritance can sometimes be complex, but is also highly rewarding.

Gaining an honorary aunt

Tim had the task of clearing a house that had been owned by Madeline, his spinster aunt, and dealing with her affairs after her death. He found a will leaving her property to close family members, but she had bequeathed some of her personal possessions, plus a sum of money, to 'my dear friend, Jennifer Williams'. Tim did not know this woman. Although he found some letters and cards signed 'love Jen', they were quite old and when he sent a letter to the address it was returned marked 'not known'. Tim's parents had died and no older relatives were left to ask. Madeline's solicitor could not help, but told Tim that Jennifer had to be located before his aunt's estate could be distributed.

Tim went to the town where Jennifer had lived and spoke to her former neighbours. He discovered that she had moved to a retirement home a few miles away. By searching the internet, he was able to locate Jennifer's building and a call to the caretaker confirmed that a woman of the right name did indeed live in the property.

Tim elected to write to Jennifer and received a phone call from her immediately. She was sad to hear of Madeline's death, but pleased to hear from Tim as she had no relatives living locally. Madeline's estate was duly distributed and all her affairs settled. Tim and his wife have now 'adopted' Jennifer as an honorary aunt – they visit her every month and take her out on day trips now and again.

Intestacy is the term used for the administration of an estate where there is no will: if someone dies without leaving a will they are said to have died 'intestate'. This is a common problem and where the deceased had assets — money or property — these need to be distributed lawfully.

Often relatives will come forward to claim the whole, or a share, of an estate. But sometimes the deceased had no close relatives or no contact with known family. If no relatives can be found, the proceeds of the estate eventually go to the government.

There are rules that determine who can inherit in cases of intestacy, depending on their relationship to the deceased. These rules can sometimes be complicated to interpret, particularly in cases where the closest relatives are very distant or there are remarriages, illegitimacy or half-relatives of any kind. The administrator of such an estate might find it difficult to identify the relatives who are entitled to inherit and then locate them to notify them of their potential inheritance.

Trust funds are drawn up for a number of reasons and often contain a clause that allows money to be paid out or property to be left to beneficiaries, either at a particular date in the future or in the event of a specific occurrence, such as the death or remarriage of a relative. When trust funds are due to pay out it is not unusual to encounter difficulties when trying to locate or contact one or more of the beneficiaries.

Finding **owners of land or property** is another request I receive fairly regularly. Someone might want to buy the property, develop land or inform the owner of illegal use or unsafe buildings. Although land ownership records exist for a large percentage of UK property, sometimes the information they contain is out of date. In other cases the ownership is disputed or leases have expired, making it necessary to renew agreements or draw up new ownership documents. See Chapter 6 for information about property ownership records.

Home sweet home

Next to the house where Robert and Judy were temporarily living was a larger property that had been empty for several years. Robert and Judy's lease was coming to an end and they were now in a position to buy somewhere to live. They liked the area and were interested in purchasing the property next door, but none of the immediate neighbours knew who the owners were.

Judy asked at the local council while Robert spoke to people locally and made enquiries at the Post Office, but neither of them made much progress. Eventually Robert was told about Land Registry records and decided to contact the organisation to see if they could help. Through the Land Registry, Robert discovered that the property owners were Diane and Oliver White, a couple who now lived in Portugal. An internet search of the address provided by the Land Registry revealed that Mr and Mrs White ran a villa complex, and the website provided a contact email for Robert White. An enquiry via this email address prompted a reply the very next day and the property sale was completed two months later.

Many people have occupational **pensions**, some that go back a number of years. Changes of employment and the passing of years often mean that the pension company or former employer is no longer in touch with the person who paid in to their pension when they reach retirement age. Unless the former employee comes forward to claim the pension – and quite a number every year forget about pensions they are entitled to – the fund holder needs to take steps to establish whether that person is still living and if so where they are.

In terms of recovering money rather than giving it out, searching for someone to recover a **debt** can also be difficult, not least because the person sought is probably not keen to be found! I choose not to undertake this type of search because the success rate can be mixed and the result is unrewarding. It is much nicer to be looking for someone for reasons that are beneficial to them in some way. There are, however, many avenues that you can try (see Chapters 2 to 9).

If the debt is substantial or important you may wish to consider using the services of a specialist investigator (see Chapter 8 for more information).

Finding the Best Way

The reasons for wanting to find another person or research your family are, as you can now see, as varied as the individuals themselves. As the reasons are different, so are the solutions: each case has its own unique background, research path and outcome. The following chapters focus on the range of resources available for finding people, so that you can identify the best way for you to search and reunite with anyone you have lost.

Chapter Two

MAKING A START

There are six important things to do before you start a search.

Think About the Person, Jog Your Own Memory

Thinking about the person that you would like to find for a few days before you start your search can help to jog your memory, particularly if you have not seen this person for many years.

Write down every single thing you can remember, including their name, age, birthday, occupation, hobbies, where they used to live, the names of other family members and so on. This process may take several days, but write down every detail, including things that may not seem relevant. Once you are sure you have as much detail as possible, reading through this book will help you to decide where to start and which avenues are likely to be most productive.

Think Carefully About Your Reasons

Next, consider your reason for wanting to locate this person. It may be for a particular occasion, such as a school reunion, significant birthday or anniversary. If this is the case allow plenty of time, as finding someone can sometimes take many months.

People often decide to seek someone from their past – a relative, old friend or lost sweetheart – at times when life has changed in some way. The birth of a child often prompts us to think about family bonds and wonder about our own blood relatives. The loss of a loved one usually leads to thoughts of our own mortality and the realisation that there may be limited time to seek out or catch up with friends and family.

Nostalgia can sometimes be quite overwhelming, for example finding an old photograph that kindles fond memories. Loneliness can also be a reason for seeking out family members or friends from the past.

Dissatisfaction with the current life, whether subconscious or acknowledged, can lead to longing for a different life, perhaps one that existed many years ago. There might also be a yearning to rekindle carefree feelings of youth in times when life becomes fraught with problems and responsibilities.

Reality check

Gina had started thinking about Roger, her neighbour and friend throughout her childhood, when she had been married for 11 years. Digging through old photographs to put them in an album, Gina found several pictures of her and Roger as children. She had fond memories of him and when they were teenagers there had even been a hint of romance.

Bored with her life and wanting some excitement, Gina tracked Roger down on the internet and they exchanged many messages over the course of a few weeks. They arranged to meet in secret, not wishing to upset their spouses. Gina remembered a good-looking, interesting, fun young man, but the reality of Roger in his mid-40s did not live up to this. He was overweight, had lost most of his hair, and had become a rather self-obsessed middle-aged man.

This was a reality check for Gina, which caused her to consider what was lacking in her life and her marriage. She promised herself that she would resolve her current problems, make more effort with her husband – and never try to track down men from her past again.

Occasionally I hear stories of a desire for revenge or to settle a score from years ago. In cases like these I would usually recommend counselling to talk through feelings of bitterness or regret, rather than acting on those feelings!

Consider Your Expectations

When you have established your reason for wanting to find someone, it is important to consider your expectations and prepare for every possible outcome.

A father you haven't seen since your childhood may be overjoyed to hear from his long-lost child; he might equally be hostile or indifferent, especially if he is now in a relationship with someone who has no knowledge of his former life.

A teenager who ran away from home may be full of regret after a few years and longing to hear from their parents or siblings; they might equally have made a new life and not wish to be reminded of the old one.

An old school friend might be delighted to have contact from a former classmate; or may not, for whatever reason, wish to reminisce or reunite.

Consider also that the person you want to find may have died. This would be a sad discovery, but it would be much worse if it followed months of searching filled with the hope of a happy reunion.

Ensure You Have Emotional Support

Undertaking a search, whether for a family member or a significant person from your past, can be an emotional, even traumatic experience. Memories, nostalgia, feelings of resentment or abandonment, yearning for lost youth and regret for what might have been are common feelings that can arise. I have spent many hours listening to clients who are deciding whether or not to search, examining their reasons, talking through their fears, joining in the joy of reunion or picking up the pieces if things don't work out as they hoped. Some searches, such as those for a natural parent, are 'once in a lifetime' journeys and their importance cannot be underestimated. Waiting for news, fear, anticipation and possible rejection should not be endured alone.

Before making a firm decision, talk to relatives or close friends, go through the possible options, ask them to support you throughout the process, and reassure yourself that there will be others around to comfort you if things go wrong. If you have no close family or trusted friends, perhaps you could approach a counsellor, vicar or social worker if you have one.

Anticipate Moral Dilemmas

Many searches have potential moral dilemmas, some that are obvious even before you start a search and some that become apparent later. This is one of the most difficult parts of my job: helping people make decisions that will affect not just themselves but the life and family of the person they are seeking. Often there is no obvious right or wrong decision and anticipating every possible outcome, weighing up the advantages and disadvantages, needs to be given due time and thought.

Children seeking natural parents who have new lives and families is a common scenario – a daughter who has not seen her father since childhood, for example. Another is a parent who left a child but wants to re-establish contact now that the son or daughter is an adult. Long-lost loves present a range of dilemmas, particularly as the person sought is likely to be in a relationship.

To tell or not to tell?

When Pat's mother Margaret was a teenager during the war, there was an army camp near to her village in Scotland. Baby Pat was born to a barely 16-year-old Margaret and raised by her grandparents, being told that they were her parents and Margaret was her older sister. Margaret left home when Pat was just 9 and moved to the south coast of England, where she married and had two further daughters.

When Pat was in her late 30s the people she had always thought were her parents died within a year of each other. She attempted to contact Margaret, but received no reply to her letter and later found out that Margaret had also died. Pat was a little sad, but had seen her only rarely and because of their age difference they had had little in common. But Pat was in for a shock that she could never have imagined, when she discovered that the wills of her 'parents' both stated that Margaret was their daughter and Pat was in fact their granddaughter.

Pat hastily obtained a copy of her full birth certificate, which established as a fact that Margaret was her mother! With this revelation came a dilemma: should she tell Margaret's other daughters that she was actually their sister, not their aunt? She had seen them as young children and remembered them fondly, although she did not know them well. She asked me to find out their addresses, which I did, but she did not have the courage to make contact and tell them the full story.

In the end an opportunity came up when, almost a year later, Margaret's daughter Denise decided to research her family tree and wrote to Pat for information. After a few letters and phone calls, a visit was arranged and Pat chose to reveal the truth. Although the news was a shock, Denise took it well and she and Pat are now firm friends as well as new-found sisters. The other sister did not find it so easy to accept the situation and became immensely jealous of the close relationship Pat and Denise had formed. She is no longer in touch with either of her sisters.

Set a Budget

It is also a good idea at this stage to decide how much money you are willing to spend on your search and set some sort of budget. It is easy to get carried away and keep trying increasingly expensive methods if you are not successful at first. Obviously a search for a natural parent or sibling is going to be worth investing more money in than you might be prepared to spend on tracing a school friend, former neighbour or long-lost second cousin.

If you're undertaking a search yourself, it is possible you will be lucky and find the right person without any financial outlay, or it may only cost a few pounds. However, searches can escalate in cost if you need to use chargeable internet resources or start ordering document copies to discover more information.

If you have no luck on your own, you may decide that professional assistance is required. Consider first the non-profit agencies who offer a fixed-fee service (see Chapter 8). Traceline, for example, currently charges a total of around £60 and the Salvation Army offers a subsidised service for £40. (All costs given in this book are correct at the time of writing but are obviously subject to change.)

Private tracing services are more expensive, and complex searches, especially where contact has been lost for many years, can reach hundreds of pounds, occasionally more. It is important to tell your researcher or investigator your maximum budget and try to obtain a firm quote or accurate estimate before committing yourself to an agreement.

Establish the Facts

You need to establish the true facts – don't take family information for granted.

When applications arrive, my first step is to verify the information provided by my client. This is not because I don't trust them or think their memory is inaccurate; it is because around six times out of ten, at least one piece of information supplied to me is incorrect. Even very close relatives can get things wrong. Aunt Mary might have been registered at birth as Alice Mary but hated the name Alice. You might be sure that your friend Michael's birthday was April 5th but actually it was May 4th. You're certain your cousin Sylvia lived at number 122 (actually it was 112). Your father Tony may have been called William after his grandfather but used Tony as a nickname because he liked it better. Even if you knew someone quite well, feel sure that you remember their exact age, are certain of their birthday and know the address where they lived, check and double check the information before embarking on a search that may be long, complex and potentially expensive.

The following case study provides a salutary lesson in the importance of checking carefully all the details you have.

Check your facts

Cherry contacted me from the US to ask for help with locating relatives of her mother, Annie, who had died the previous year. Annie had suffered from dementia for a number of years and the family papers had all been lost, but Cherry knew that her mother had four sisters and was hopeful of finding her aunts and some cousins.

She had tried hard to find out what she could from a distance, and had even managed to obtain a copy of her mother's birth certificate, which she sent to me with her application. Feeling sure that Cherry would know the details, I did not question whether the birth certificate was correct.

After months of complicated research I traced a nephew of the Annie on the certificate and explained to him what I was trying to find out. To my surprise, and Cherry's disappointment, he informed me that his aunt Annie was alive and well, running a fish-and-chip shop in the town where she was born. She had never even travelled out of the country. It transpired that the certificate Cherry had given me wasn't her mother's birth certificate: it related to a woman with the same name of the same age who was born in the same region. When I reported the news to Cherry that we had been researching the wrong family, she said, 'I wondered why that certificate had the wrong birthday...'

Check **spellings, middle names and nicknames**. Do you know someone who doesn't use their real first name in everyday life? When I asked this question in a family research workshop, 20 out of 31 people raised their hands. There are two examples within my own family: my mother is always called by her middle name and an uncle was always known by his nickname. This is why the first thing I often do when starting a new case is to obtain the birth certificate of the person being sought to verify their exact name and the correct spelling. Read about how to apply for certificates in Chapter 5.

Checking the information you remember can be done in a number of ways:

* Dig out old address books, records or photographs that might have the correct information.
* Ask anyone else who knew the person or people you are looking for what they remember, to see if their facts correspond with yours.
* Locate the historical electoral registers for the address where the person lived – this may also give you information about their family (see Chapter 6).
* Certificates of life events – birth, marriage and death – relating to the person and their family can provide important information (see Chapter 5).
* Old telephone directories can confirm the correct surname and former address (see later in this chapter).

With a little help from my friends

Jon was organising a college reunion for the class of 1955. He was in touch with three fellow graduates – two men and a woman – and through word of mouth and simple procedures they were able to locate six more. This is when Jon came to me with a list of names and a target of 30 people to find within three months. The information he provided, however, was very sketchy with lots of question marks! He was also on a budget. I suggested that he and his friends try to come up with more information.

Jon managed to obtain from the college a list of stu-
dents who had been in their year. The friends arranged to
meet for lunch at his house, bringing photographs, old
papers and memorabilia from their college years. They dis-
cussed their fellow graduates one by one, gradually coming
up with further snippets of information: the road one person
lived in, the name of someone's brother, the month of one
girl's birthday, the occupation of one boy's father. At the
local library, they checked old electoral registers and phone
directories. I was able to use this additional information to
identify the correct details for 18 more individuals, 16 of
whom were located in time for the reunion.

Simple Things to Try

Easy things sometimes do work, a fact that can be overlooked if you're anticipating a long and complex search. A
few times I have received applications for searches then
found details of the person being sought within ten minutes, in the first place I looked. The clients have been surprised that it was so quick and simple.

Try some of the steps below before you think about
asking for professional help.

The local **phone book** for the area where you think
the person lives is a good start — if they live in the same
region as you, the information you're seeking could be in
your own living room! BT's online directory enquiries
service at www.bt.com/directory-enquiries covers the
whole of the UK and allows unlimited free searches for
personal use. Simply phoning round same-surname

households within an area sometimes finds a helpful relative who is willing to pass a message to the person you are
seeking.

If you don't have access to the internet there are a
large number of telephone directory enquiries services to
choose from, including the ones below. These are in no
particular order (costs per enquiry apply to calls from a
landline):

* 118 500 (BT) – 49p connection charge + 24p/min.
* 118 118 (The Number) – 59p connection charge +
  14p/min.
* 118 878 (NTL) – 40p connection charge + 23p/min.
* 118 114 (Co op) – 40p per call.
* 118 000 (Orange) – 49p connection charge +
  24p/min.
* 118 811 (One) – 40p per call (one number).
* 118 499 (Share) – 49p connection charge + 9p/min
  (max. 2 enquiries; 5p from each call goes to charity).

Please note that you will usually need to give a surname
and town of residence (Orange also requires the street
address) to obtain a phone number. Read more about telephone directories, where to find them and how to look up
historical records of telephone numbers in Chapter 6.

Even if the person or family you are seeking has
moved, their **last known address** can still lead to them.
Sometimes the current residents have a forwarding
address. Former neighbours might have remained in touch
or be able to tell you more about where they moved to.

Neighbourliness

Rita asked me to find her cousin Dana after a Christmas card she had sent was returned marked 'gone away'. A long search located Dana's brother, who told Rita that Dana had moved to New Zealand.

When Dana was contacted she was surprised to learn that Rita had paid a researcher to find her. The current resident of her old house knew she had gone abroad, and both her former neighbours, who were very good friends, had her address and phone number and she is still regularly in touch with them.

If at first you are unable to find a certain individual, the **family and friends** of the person you are looking for can often come to the rescue. Parents may still live in the same area, perhaps even the same house, as the person grew up in. Their brothers or sisters might also have remained in the area. Think about mutual friends who might know where the person is, or be able to tell you more about the family after you lost touch. Ask questions – even if someone isn't still in touch with the person you're looking for, they could tell you some detail that might make your search easier or quicker.

Old school friends

Dave and Chris had been friends throughout secondary school, after sitting together on the first day. 'We hit it off straight away,' says Chris, 'and we had lots of mutual interests.' They spent a great deal of time at each other's homes and saw each other regularly throughout their late teens, but when they were both 20 Chris left the area to study, then relocated to another part of the country to work. The two remained in touch until an email sent to Dave's work address was returned.

'I called his office but they told me he had left five months ago,' said Chris. 'They wouldn't tell me where he had gone due to data protection and at that stage I felt pretty stuck.'

Chris knew that Dave's parents had moved when they divorced but he didn't know their new addresses. Luckily, Chris remembered Dave's father's first name and looked for likely entries in the online telephone directory. His second call led to Dave's father, who was more than happy to give Chris the new address and phone number.

If the person you are looking for is a former college or university friend, try the **alumni association** for the institution you attended – your friend may be a member. You could call the college or university and ask for the alumni office, or type the name of the place or institution plus the word 'alumni' into your internet browser (e.g. 'Manchester University Alumni').

Alternatively, www.alumni.net lists educational institutions worldwide, but you will need to register with the site to view and exchange information.

Once you've exhausted these simple suggestions, Chapter 3 outlines what to try next.

Chapter Three

WHAT TO TRY NEXT

If looking in the phone book or asking family and friends gets you nowhere, there are other avenues you can pursue to progress your search.

Online Searches

At present there are two main services offering online searches for UK residents. Both are based on the electoral register and telephone directory, with some additional information and features.

192.com is an established online service with phone directory, electoral register and company director information. Searches are free, but you need to purchase credits to obtain the results (starting from £34.95 for 100 credits valid for six months). For premium information such as historical electoral registers an extra annual fee of £149.99 is payable.

192 is now also available on www.findmypast.com (sign in and click on the 'Living Relatives' link). The current cost per search on this service is 10 units (approx £1).

Tracesmart (www.tracesmart.co.uk) is one of my favourite sites; I use it almost daily. It combines current and recent electoral register data, telephone listings, details of company directors, property ownership

Tracesmart.co.uk is highly recommended and cost effective.
© 2006 Tracesmart Ltd

information and much more in the form of the Tracesmart register. Options also include multiple name searches to identify couples and families living together and reverse searching by address.

Initial searches are free and help you to identify the number of matches before you pay to view the results. Prices start from under £20 and there are a number of flexible options, including one credit for £14.95 or a 24-

hour pass for £24.95 giving you unlimited searching. Multiple credits can be purchased at a discount.

When you're faced with pages or dozens of matches for a particular name, how can you tell which entry is the right one? Clients of mine often try an internet search themselves but become stuck when they get back numerous possible addresses because the name they are searching on is quite common.

There are several ways to narrow down a list of results, depending on how much information you have about the person you would like to find:

* Geographical area
* Middle initial
* Other occupants
* Age
* Type of accommodation

You can restrict your search to a particular **town, county, city or postcode area**, which is a useful option if you have an idea of where the person lives.

Middle names or initials can be ascertained through birth or marriage certificates, former electoral register entries from old addresses, or other public and family resources. Tracesmart has an option to search only for people with a particular middle initial.

The middle initial
Daniel had wanted to find his father John for several years and had tried a few times without success. He had searched

online directories and registers, but given up because his father's name was too common.

A colleague told Daniel about Tracesmart. When he entered his father's name there were 76 matches, but more than half could be eliminated because they had a different middle initial. Checking the remaining entries, Daniel found three that could relate to his father in terms of age.

One of these entries was for a man living in the area where John was last known to have been working. A short note to the address resulted in father and son being in contact after 17 years.

Couples are far easier to pin down than individuals. There might be hundreds of entries for Sally Johnson or Paul Johnson, for example, but a manageable number of couples called Sally and Paul Johnson. Both Tracesmart and 192 have a family or combined name search option.

It used to be a matter of course that the wife took her husband's **surname** when they married. This identified them as a couple and made research easier because there were almost no exceptions. During the mid- to late-twentieth century this started to change, however. More women now keep their maiden name when they get married. Some say that they don't want to feel 'owned' by their husband, others that they have gained recognition or qualifications under their own surname or that it would just be too complicated to change everything.

Some couples even decide to adopt the wife's surname instead, particularly if they have children and want to be identified as a family unit but the husband's surname is unsuitable for some reason.

Another choice that couples have made is to hyphenate their surnames to form a new one.

No more Mrs Jones

Mike and Andrea met at college and fell madly in love, and by the age of 19 both were sure that they wanted to spend the rest of their lives together. The only problem was Mike's surname: Jones. Andrea did not want to be 'Mrs Jones' and was rather attached to her own surname, Harding.

Their solution was for Mike to change his surname by deed poll to Harding-Jones before their marriage, then when they married his wife automatically became 'Mrs Harding-Jones'.

When married women divorce, more than ever before they are opting to revert to their maiden name, causing yet more confusion for researchers. After a marriage has ended it is understandable that an ex-husband's surname is a constant reminder and discarding this is a way of moving on from the marriage. This can all mean that you have to think laterally when trying to find people who may have married or divorced.

Ages are not recorded for electoral purposes, but a great number of Tracesmart entries have dates of birth associated with individuals at particular addresses. Even if you do not find a named person of the right age, many entries can be eliminated because they are completely the wrong age.

Addresses in the UK today are categorised by a sophisticated process called **social profiling**, which is used for marketing purposes. Tracesmart provides a Mosaic social profile with all its entry results. If you are looking for a retired banker, for example, he or she is unlikely to be living in a council flat in an area where most residents are claiming benefits. Likewise, a street cleaner or waiter would probably not live in a road where residences are classed as 'symbols of success'.

Letters to Same-Surname Households

This is a method that sometimes works well and can bring results with very little outlay. It is most successful if you know the specific area that a person came from and if their surname is not too common. Writing to all the Jones families in Cardiff is probably not going to help, but writing to all the Westbrook families in the Bournemouth area is quite likely to find someone who is related and can get a message to the person you are seeking.

Lists of residents in an area can be obtained simply by going through the phone book or accessing online directory enquiries listings for the area. Although this is free, it can miss a high percentage of residents due to unlisted phone numbers. Combining phone listings with electoral register entries is an effective way of identifying a higher percentage of residents in an area (see above).

The way you write your letter can influence the number of responses you receive and whether or not your appeal ends up in the bin. A good speculative letter will include information about you, the person you are seeking and your reason for wanting to get in touch with them. It is also a nice idea to include a first-class stamp to cover the cost of a reply or phone call. Don't forget to supply as much contact information for yourself as possible, including postal address, home and work phone numbers, mobile number and email addresses.

Dear Mrs Browning

I am looking for a lady called Vera Willis, last known to be living in the Cheltenham area in the early to mid-1970s. She was my mother's former neighbour and they were very good friends at the time. Vera was born around 1936, possibly in the Stroud area, and her maiden name was Browning.

Her parents were William and Florence Browning and her father was a bus driver. Vera married in 1955 to Sid Hancock — my mother attended the wedding (picture of bride and groom enclosed).

My mum has been in hospital for a few weeks following a fall. She is now at home recovering and would very much like to write to her old friend. I am therefore contacting all of the Browning households in Cheltenham and surrounding areas in the hope that I might find a relative of Vera.

If you have any connection with Vera, even if you do not know her current whereabouts, please do get in touch. You are welcome to call me if you have any questions.

I am enclosing a self-addressed envelope and a first-class stamp to cover the cost of a letter or phone call.

Thank you for your help. I look forward to hearing from you soon.

Yours sincerely

Example of a letter to a possible relative

Using the media

The media have always been very helpful when it comes to searching for lost relatives. Human interest stories are something that readers, viewers and listeners never seem to tire of. You don't need to get on to national television to reach a large number of people – local services can be just as effective.

Thousands of press releases are received every day in the offices of **national newspapers** and it can be difficult to get your correspondence noticed. It is possible, if there is a strong human interest hook (dying reader needs bone-marrow transplant, for example), but your search for a lost auntie would probably not get any attention. Some national papers, including the *Daily Mail,* do have sections where they print appeals from readers.

Many **local newspapers** have a regular section in which they feature appeals for missing relatives and lost friends. The one pictured opposite, which used to feature regularly in the *Southern Daily Echo,* is typical. Many local papers also have an online version, where readers can search archives and even submit appeals.

There are a number of resources to help you find the newspaper that covers the area the person you are seeking comes from or is thought to be living.

Willings Press Guide lists information about and contact details for publications in the UK, including all local and regional newspapers. You can search by the name of the paper or geographically by the county, town, region or city it covers.

Searchline

Lt Cromwell Varley

IN 1990 a diver discovered the wreck of the submarine H5 off the coast of Anglesey, North Wales. H5 was built in Montreal, Canada, in 1915, and on arriving in Britain was stationed on the East Coast where it sank the German submarine U51 in 1916. From 1915 until her transfer to Ireland in 1917 she was commanded by Lt Cromwell H Varley, DSC. She was then commanded by Lt A W Forbes, DSO, until her loss in 1918.
Lt Varley remained in the Royal Navy until 1930, by when he had risen to the rank of commander.
He later founded Varley Marine, based at Locks Heath, near Southampton, where he did development and experimental work on the midget submarines.
If anyone has information on Commander Varley after he left the Navy or who worked for Varley Marine prior to the Second World War I would be grateful if they would contact me. I would also like to know what became of Commander Varley after the war. The crew are commemorated on the Portsmouth Naval Memorial.
MICHAEL BOWYER, 2 Ty Ceffyl Mor, Porth Penrhyn, Bangor, Gwynedd, LL57 4HN. Phone/fax 01248 351898.

John Phillip Smith

I WOULD like to trace my half-brother John Phillip Smith who was born on July 31, 1949. He was adopted by a farming family at the age of two weeks and moved from New Romney in Kent to Somerset. They subsequently moved to the New Forest area.
W E SMITH, 153, Poltingfield Road, Rye, East Sussex TN31 7BW 01797 225192.

Gregory family

WE are planning a family reunion in Australia on January 14, 2002.
I would like to trace relatives of William and Louisa Newell (nee Gregory) from Eling, Totton, who married in July 1864. Their children were: William, twins Richard and George, Elizabeth, Fred, Annie (emigrated to Australia in the 1900s), Harry (went to Canada), Charles, Louisa (married de Lacy then went to Australia) and John.
Edith Annie Holmes, born 1876, lived in Goodworth Clatford and Alresford then emigrated to Western Australia in 1912.
KATH BOLIN, 18 Towning Street, Embleton 6062, Western Australia. e-mail: bolinr@iexpress.net.au

Edward Tom Taylor

MY father died when I was very young and I would like to trace anyone who knew him. His name was Edward Tom Taylor and he served in the Second Battalion Dorset Regiment.
He was based in Nowshera, India, and travelled there on HMT Lancashire via Gibraltar, Malta, Port Said and Aden finally disembarking at Karachi in 1939. Does anyone know of any association which may have records of my father?
MICK TAYLOR, 17 Whitebeam Road, Hedge End, Southampton SO30 0PZ.

Mandy Norris

IN 1987, I was a sergeant in the United States Marine Corps. While visiting Benidorm, Spain, I met a young lady from Southampton. Her name was Mandy Norris. I would like to hear from her.
LeROY ACOSTA, San Diego, California USA. e-mail: leroyacosta@hotmail.com

Southern Daily Echo, 22 June 2000

A copy of *Willings Press Guide* can be found in almost every public library, except very small branches. The copy held may not be the most recent, but the information will probably still be current. See www.willingspress.com for more information about this directory.

Another way to find contact details for local newspapers is to search **online lists**. You could try entering likely terms such as 'Salisbury local newspaper' – Google's top result is the *Salisbury Journal*. There are also specific lists of local newspapers by name. A typical example is www.onlinenewspapers.com, which is quite comprehensive. It features newspapers worldwide, but for the UK its list includes:

✳   England A–K
✳   England L–Z
✳   Scotland
✳   Wales

There is a separate site for Ireland.

A number of **magazines** feature a section devoted to reuniting loved ones, particularly those whose target audience is the older generation, such as *Saga* and *Choice*. The latter is a glossy magazine for the 'young retired' market and has an established UK readership. It features a monthly 'Get in Touch' column, where appeals for lost family and friends and reunion notices are published (see opposite). This is a free service, but there is a long waiting list. Call 01733 555123 for enquiries or 01858 438859 for subscriptions.

Other magazines, particularly if there is a strong human interest element to your story, may be willing to feature an article about your search for someone. Write to the editor with the details, including who you are looking for, how you lost touch, your reason for wanting to find them and so on, and you may well be rewarded with a free national appeal.

You could also try a **radio appeal.** As with newspapers, you are more likely to have an appeal broadcast on a local station than a national one. Details of local BBC stations can be found on www.bbc.co.uk/radio, or look in your local Yellow Pages under 'Broadcasting services'.

Some national shows do broadcast appeals for lost loves and relatives, including BBC Radio 2's *Sunday Love*

A 'Get in Touch' page from *Choice*.

Choice Magazine, First Floor, 2 King Street, Peterborough PE1 1LT

tel: 01733 555123, email: editorial@choicemag.co.uk.

Songs hosted by Steve Wright. Read more about the show on the BBC website at www.bbc.co.uk/radio2/shows/sunlovesongs/lostloves.shtml or tune in at 9 a.m. on a Sunday morning.

If you have an urgent situation and need to contact someone who is away from home or whose whereabouts are unknown, the BBC will sometimes help. The *Today* programme on BBC Radio 4 on weekday mornings occasionally broadcasts appeals for people to get in touch. This service is only available in cases of extreme family emergency, such as a gravely ill relative.

Long before the internet, services such as **Teletext** via your television set were giving information about a wide range of subjects. This includes one that is now well established, helping people to reunite with friends and relatives.

The 'Connect' service is on Channel 4, Teletext pages 170–179, with options to look for friends and family, service pals and those who share your family history. Page numbers may change in the future, particularly when analogue television is completely replaced by digital.

A Teletext page.

Chapter Four

WAYS TO USE THE WEB

Since the beginning of the internet there have been numerous directories of people, addresses, phone numbers and email addresses. Some have survived and grown, others have been incomplete and poorly maintained, and some have been discontinued.

Email Directories

Directories of email addresses are notoriously difficult to compile and maintain. Information about personal email addresses can be gathered from various sources, but no directory is completely comprehensive. Also, due to changes in employers, computers or internet service providers, email addresses inevitably change quite frequently.

The **Ultimate Email Directory** (www.theultimates. com/email/) is a common interface to six online email directories, including Yahoo and Bigfoot.

The **Free Email Search** website (www.free-emailsearch.com) also checks numerous search engines and directories for email addresses.

Search Engines

Ordinary search engines can be overlooked as a resource when trying to trace someone, but the advanced way that information is collected from the sites they list means that details can be found without the need to search individual websites. For example, if the person you are looking for is an employee, partner or proprietor of a business, their name and sometimes their picture may be featured on that organisation's website. This works well, particularly if the person has an unusual name or an uncommon combination of forename and surname.

Meet the ABC Team (left to right): Paul Cassidy, Steve Castle, John O'Roarke, Peter Horton and Phil Bunker. Photograph copyright Marie-Ange Bouchard 2006

© www.abcinsurance.co.uk, reproduced by permission.

Google (www.google.co.uk) can be a straightforward and useful tool if you need to find information quickly.

An unusual surname

Sarah discovered quite late in life that she was adopted. She had never questioned whether the people looking after her were her parents but, when they died within a year of each other, letters and papers came to light that revealed the truth.

Sarah pieced together her story. Registered at birth as Alice, she lived with her mother Judith and sister Victoria until she was almost a year old. Judith's husband William had been away at war for two years when Alice was born, the result of an affair with a man who was also married. William forgave his wife, but insisted that it was impossible for another man's child to remain in the family. Judith faced the difficult decision to give up her baby in order to save her marriage.

Alice was finally adopted when she was 11 months old and renamed Sarah. Despite exhaustive searches, no record of Judith, her husband or daughter could be found. Even Judith's parents seemed to have disappeared and their deaths were not recorded in the UK.

Sarah was starting to give up hope, but her grandparents had a very uncommon surname. She trawled the internet for any mention of this name and checked all the references. Several entries had connections with South Africa, one with an email address. A discreet message followed by tentative exchanges revealed that the man in question was Judith's nephew. Later came the news that Judith was still alive and contact was established between Sarah, her mother and her sister Victoria. They exchanged letters and at the time of writing plans are being made for Sarah to visit her family in South Africa.

Metacrawler (www.metacrawler.com) is another of my favourite sites. Metacrawler checks search engines and millions of websites worldwide in an instant for names, words or phrases that may help you to find someone. Combining a name with a profession, job title or hobby helps to limit the results. Putting the forename and surname in inverted commas also makes results more relevant, since you only get entries that contain that combination.

For example, say you are looking for an old friend called Heather White. You have heard that she is doing well in her career working in the field of business coaching and networking. If you entered the terms coach, networking and 'Heather White', the second, fourth and fifth results listed would find your friend:

2.
CMM business speaker list. Speakers corporate workshops ...
Mairi Watson – Work life balance coach ... Heather White – The Magic of Networking, Heather White. Simon Woodroffe – YO! Sushi Entrepreneur ...
www.cmmol.net/business_speakers.htm [Found on Google, Yahoo! Search, Ask.com]
4.
Heather White – Business Speaker, Networking Consultant
Heather White is a professional networker who helps businesses gain 100% more from their networking investment. She is a speaker, trainer, coach and author. ...
www.cityspeakersinternational.co.uk/speakers/speak... [Found on Google, Yahoo! Search]
5.
The Magic of Networking
Why do you want to network? Skills, behaviours and strategies. How we can deliver networking "Magic"! And how you can believe. About Heather White. About Heather White. "If she can do it, y...
www.magicof.co.uk/aboutheatherwhite.html [Found on Yahoo! Search, Ask.com]

Message Board Sites

The message board set-up was the first way in which people were reunited with each other using the internet. The idea is simple: messages and appeals are posted by individuals looking for others, and these can be read by anyone who visits the site. If this includes the person being sought, or someone who knows them, the seeker and the sought can be reunited. Some sites, including 'Missing You', also have a search facility so that visitors don't need to trawl through pages of appeals to discover if there is a message regarding a particular person.

Missing You (www.missing-you.net) remains one of the few genuinely free message board sites for finding

people. It attracts around 25,000 visitors per month from the UK and overseas and has successfully reunited hundreds of relatives and friends. Registration in order to post an appeal is easy; this also allows confidential messaging between users. Select from a number of options including region and category. As soon as your appeal is submitted it will appear on the site.

Reunite Sites

Friends Reunited and Genes Reunited are extremely successful sites that have helped to reunite numerous friends and relatives. The chances are high that the person you are looking for, one of their relatives or someone who is in touch with them is a member of one of these sites.

Friends Reunited (www.friendsreunited.co.uk), established in 1999, was a revelation. Eight years on it has a staggering 14 million members, proving that there is a fundamental need for many people to remain in touch with their childhood and teenage friends throughout life.

If you want to make contact with school, college, university or workplace friends, the easy registration and nominal membership fee are well worth investing in. Basic registration is free and, once you have registered, your details will appear on the site for your old friends and colleagues to see and you will also be able to look for friends and view their profiles. If you want then to upgrade to full membership (currently under £15 per year), you will be able to send messages to anyone you find on the site.

The concept was simple, membership was cheap and the site attracted not just millions of visitors but also media attention. © www.friendsreunited.co.uk.

There are also message board facilities to post requests if you are trying to find someone, and a name search facility to look for people you know but didn't attend school with.

Genes Reunited (www.genesreunited.co.uk) is fast catching up with its sister site, Friends Reunited, in membership. In terms of individual names listed on the site, the figure now stands at over 70 million.

© www.genesreunited.co.uk

The concept grasped by the founders of Genes Reunited (formerly Genes Connected) is that living relatives who share the same ancestor may want to link up with each other for their mutual benefit. I have found several distant 'cousins' using the site and we have exchanged photographs, compared family traits and pooled our research. This concept can not only save a great deal of time and money in duplicated research, but can also lead to lasting relationships.

The premise is simple: enter your details and those of all your known family members and ancestors. Other members do the same. You are then able to match up with those who share the same ancestors. This is done by either member searching for others who have entered the same details, or asking the site to check who else has the same people in their tree. There is also an automatic notification facility called 'hot matches', which sends monthly emails with details of people whose relatives are similar to any person on your tree.

Registration is free; you can then enter your family members and search for matching names. A nominal annual membership, currently under £10, allows full use of the site, including the facility to send emails to other members.

Tracey and her sisters

Tracey's parents, Majorie and Derek Pinney, split up in 1974, just before the birth of Tracey's younger sister Barbara. Derek stayed out of their lives and Majorie went on to marry again, to John. In 1989, when John made enquiries into adopting both Tracey and Barbara, they discovered that Derek had also remarried and had three more daughters, Nicola, Joanne and Lisa.

For years, Tracey remained curious about her siblings, but did not know where to start looking for them. On 20 May 2005, Tracey entered the surname Pinney into Genes Reunited and found a message from Nicola, also looking for her half-sisters, Tracey and Barbara. Within a week the five siblings were reunited. One year on and things are still going well between them all and Tracey has now met her real father for the first time in 30 years.

© www.genesreunited.co.uk.

Forces Reunited (www.forcesreunited.org.uk). This service, built over a number of years and combining with other similar sites, is now the most popular services reunion site for the UK. There are over 280,000 registered members. Basic registration is free, and this allows you to search the site for former forces colleagues. There is a nominal annual subscription, which enables members to post messages and contact other members.

Service Pals (www.servicepals.com) is another armed services website designed to reunite former colleagues. Again, basic registration is free, allowing members to browse the site, but a subscription is payable if you want to contact other members.

The **Royal British Legion**, the organisation for ex-service personnel, has more than 450,000 members. Its popular website (www.britishlegion.org.uk) features a section called 'Lost Trails', where members can post messages if they are looking for former armed services colleagues – follow the link to Lost Trails from the British Legion home page.

Family History Sites

If you are looking for living relatives, you might not think that searching for dead ancestors is a way to start. However, many people have become interested in family history over the last few years, and if you are trying to locate a relative, the chances are that they or one of their immediate family members has the genealogy bug. The internet plays a very large role in family research today and the details of many families and surnames can be found on various websites.

Rootsweb (www.rootsweb.com) claims to be the oldest and largest genealogy site on the internet. Its primary purpose is 'to connect people so that they can help each other and share genealogical research'. This is facilitated by free indexes, mailing lists, message board sites, surname interest groups and something called the 'WorldConnect Project', where family trees can be uploaded and shared.

Reuniting via the Rootsweb message board

Browsing a message board featuring my father's surname, I discovered that someone had sent in a message looking for relatives with his surname and for others in my family lineage.

I thought, 'Our family is so small, I've got to be related to this person.' With the exception of my siblings and me, all our relatives have spent time in orphanages and foster homes. Our parents were orphans raised in orphanages.

Hope-filled, I contacted the writer and discovered she was the daughter of one of my maternal first cousins. I had seen this first cousin the last time more than 50 years ago when her family was broken up due to the death of her father.

Thanks to email we established an online communication. From there, we visited for a wedding. I saw my first cousin across a hotel lobby just as she spotted me. Without a word we ran to each other and hugged. We needed no introductions, each of us look just like our mothers, who were sisters.

Since then we have stayed in touch and I have been reunited with three other cousins in the family. I am so grateful for Ancestry and RootsWeb and especially for the message boards.

Written by J. Hanley. Previously published in *RootsWeb Review*: 9 March 2005, Vol. 8, No. 10. © MyFamily.com Inc. and its subsidiaries.

People with fairly uncommon surnames can sometimes be traced through a member who has studied the name as part of their family research. The following sites have searchable indexes leading to contact details of the member with an interest in that surname. For example, if you are looking for someone with the surname Gillberry, look for an entry under this surname on the two sites below. If a member studying this name is shown, he or she may very well be related to or have more information on the person you are seeking.

GOONS (www.one-name.org) — The Guild of One-Name Studies — is an association for those researching a

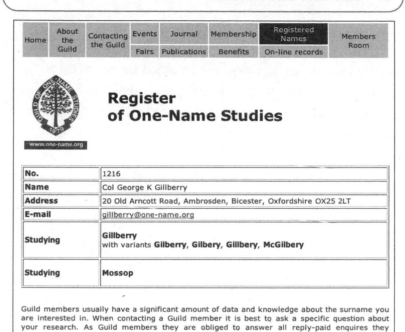

No.	1216
Name	Col George K Gillberry
Address	20 Old Arncott Road, Ambrosden, Bicester, Oxfordshire OX25 2LT
E-mail	gillberry@one-name.org
Studying	**Gillberry** with variants **Gilberry, Gilbery, Gillbery, McGilbery**
Studying	**Mossop**

Guild members usually have a significant amount of data and knowledge about the surname you are interested in. When contacting a Guild member it is best to ask a specific question about your research. As Guild members they are obliged to answer all reply-paid enquires they receive. Please see the Contacting Guild Members page on how to get in touch with the Guild member found.

Reproduced with permission from the website of the Guild of One-Name Studies, www.one-name.org.uk.

particular surname, rather than an individual family. If the person you are looking for has a surname that is studied by one of the members, they may be able to help or advise. However, do not expect a free research service: surname groups are for members to contribute and share information. If making an approach, do offer to join the group and pay an initial membership fee – this is usually nominal – or at least pay for the time and expenses of the member.

The **Online English Names Directory** (www.list. jaunay.com/engnames) is a searchable database of surname information from public submissions. A search can be made for the whole of the UK or by county. Contributors can usually be contacted by email through a link on the site, but sometimes only postal addresses are given. Be sure to follow etiquette and offer to pay expenses or, if making an approach by post, enclose a stamped addressed envelope.

The **Federation of Family History Societies** (www.ffhs.org.uk) is an umbrella organisation for all the local associations throughout the country. If the family you are searching for has strong connections with a particular geographical area, joining the association for that area could be a very good investment. Subsidised local research is often available to members and appeals for information about families can be published in the association's journal. Amateur family historians are often exceptionally helpful and may offer to look up information or write to you with memories of the family that you are trying to contact.

From the main site follow the 'Contacting our members' link, which will lead to a page of options for you to identify the society covering the area that you are interested in.

The following example from *The Hampshire Family Historian* shows that there is no substitute for local knowledge and personal contact.

The Earley family

The cover of the February 2002 issue of *The Hampshire Family Historian* featured a wedding photograph of the Earley family in the 1920s. Inside, Mrs Humby explained

THE EARLEY FAMILY
of 1920s Shirley, Southampton.

that her father, now deceased, was one of the children in the photograph. She appealed for information regarding the identity of other members of her extended family. A later issue contained a thank-you from Mrs Earley explaining how the journal had helped her link up with one of her relatives.

Queenie, her father's first cousin, was visiting her hairdresser, whose husband was a member of the society. The hairdresser also read the journal, recognised the name of her client and showed her the photograph. Queenie, then aged 85, called Mrs Humby. Aunt and niece exchanged much family information, and they were both very pleased to be in touch. Queenie was able to identify all the relatives in the photographs and she also remembered the exact date and venue of the wedding.

Reproduced with the permission of Hampshire Genealogical Society, www.hgs-online.org.uk.

Ancestry.com has been running for many years and the company has now introduced a UK version (www. ancestry.co.uk). The Ancestry database covers literally millions of records worldwide, with a high percentage of British ones. Some of the records are free to access, including birth, marriage and death indexes for England and Wales from 1837 to 1983. Short-term access to the full collection, from around £5, can be purchased through the site, or vouchers are available from a number of genealogical suppliers if you prefer to pay by cheque. Annual membership is available from £69.95 for UK records. If using Ancestry for the first time, it is useful to read the 'Search tips' section before undertaking your research.

FamilySearch (www.familysearch.org) gives you access to the resources of the largest genealogical institution in the world, The Church of Jesus Christ of the Latter Day Saints (also known as the Mormons). They have gathered and indexed millions of records from all over the world, many from the times before civil records began. Many of these are parish records of baptisms, marriages and burials. This may not seem an obvious place to look for information about the living. However, the project to collect names and data is ongoing and inclusive: anyone who has carried out their own family research is welcome to add their details and those of their living and recently deceased family members. Therefore, it is worth looking here if you are having trouble locating civil records.

Chapter 5 looks in detail at how to trace births, marriages and deaths in official indexes.

Chapter Five

TRACING BIRTHS, MARRIAGES AND DEATHS

Life events – births, marriages and deaths – in England and Wales are recorded by the General Register Office. Although changes are proposed to the way events can be registered and how much information is made available, at present these events are recorded by district register offices and made available to the public with limited restrictions.

Periodically, copies of the registers of births, marriages and deaths that have occurred locally are sent to the General Register Office, where they are indexed. These indexes, when complete for the whole country, are then made available to the public.

Until the end of 1983 the alphabetical indexes for each event were compiled quarterly and at present are available only by searching the volume for each quarter. From 1984 there are annual indexes.

The large volumes containing General Register Office indexes are held at the Family Records Centre in London. For details, see www.familyrecords.gov.uk/frc, or contact:

The Family Records Centre
1 Myddelton Street
London EC1R 1UW
Tel: 0845 603 7788

You can visit the Family Records Centre in person and do not need to book an appointment, but the building can get very busy, with lots of people carrying out research.

Alternatively, you can search the indexes online. With events from 1984 onwards it is possible to search for an event without knowing the year, but from 1837 to 1983 you need to search each individual quarter.

One of the main sites delivering online access to the General Register Office indexes is www.findmypast.com. You will need to register and purchase 'units' (minimum £5 for 50 units, or you can buy a subscription for unlimited use from £50 a year), but that can work out far cheaper than visiting the Family Records Centre in person.

Interpreting the Indexes

When you have selected the event and dates that you wish to search, the pages of entries can seem a little confusing, with lots of columns, abbreviations and codes.

Birth indexes are arranged alphabetically by surname. The columns show the following information:

* Surname
* First name
* Middle initials
* Mother's maiden name (if the mother is unmarried this will usually be the same as the mother's surname)
* District where the child was born
* District code and page number

An example of a birth index. © Crown Copyright. Published by permission of HMSO and the Office for National Statistics.

Marriage indexes should contain corresponding entries for both the bride and the groom. The columns show:

* Surname
* First name
* Middle initials
* Surname of spouse
* District where the marriage took place
* District code and page number

Death indexes can help not only establish whether someone has died, but also if they were the right age to be a member of the family you are seeking. Information is shown as follows:

An example of a marriage index. © Crown Copyright. Published by permission of HMSO and the Office for National Statistics.

An example of a death index. © Crown Copyright. Published by permission of HMSO and the Office for National Statistics.

✻   Surname
✻   First name
✻   First middle name
✻   Any second middle initial
✻   Age at death (later indexes show actual date of birth)
✻   District in which the death took place (this is not necessarily where the deceased lived, deaths have to be registered in the district where the person died)
✻   District code and page number

Knowing what happened

Jamie's mum Jane had wanted to find her older brother, Len, for quite a while. He had left the family home to work in the merchant navy a long time ago, but was not much good at keeping in touch. After a couple of years and just a handful of letters from all over the world, he stopped writing.

It was when Jane was clearing her parents' house after they died that she came across her brother's letters and some documents, including his birth certificate. She vowed she would find him, but kept meeting with obstacles.

Jamie decided to help look for his uncle in the hope of surprising his mother. Having no luck with electoral registers and message board sites, he checked the index of deaths at www.findmypast.com, not really expecting to find anything. One entry immediately leapt off the page:

Name	Date of Birth	Registration District	Year of Registration	Month of Registration
WILLIAMS, Leonard Haye	23 Nov 1932	Portsmouth	1989	April

Jamie was sure that this was his lost uncle: his grand-mother's maiden name was Haye and this was also his mother's middle name. He sneaked a look at his uncle's birth certificate to confirm that the date of birth matched, then ordered the death certificate.

Len's death had been registered by a friend and neigh-bour called Jimmy. Jimmy was contacted and told Jamie all about Len's life and the circumstances of his death. Telling Jane was not easy – she was very upset – but at least they now know what happened to uncle Len.

How to Order Certificates

If you need to find out more about the event you are interested in, you can place an application for the certificate once you have found a likely index entry for the event in question. The cost of a full certificate is currently from £7 to £11.50 depending on how it is ordered and how much information you have about the event.

Certificates can be ordered from the General Register Office in person, online, by telephone, post or fax, or from the relevant district register office.

To obtain a certificate **in person** at the Family Records Centre, complete a birth, marriage or death certificate application form, together with all the codes from the index entry, then submit your application at the payment desk. You can ask to collect the certificate or have it posted to you.

The General Register Office **online** ordering procedure is now well established. From the home page (www.gro.gov.uk), click on the 'Ordering certificates online' shortcut, then 'Order a certificate online now'. This will take you to a log-in page. Unless you will be ordering certificates regularly, click on 'Guest Login' and follow the simple procedure by entering all the details you know about the event. It is best, when using this service, if you have a reference number from the GRO index, but this is not essential, particularly if you know the exact date of the event.

Telephone orders can be placed using a credit or debit card. You will need to have as much relevant information to hand as possible, as well as any index entry details, before you call. The certificate order line is 0845 603 7788 and is available Monday to Friday 8 a.m. to 8 p.m. and Saturday 9 a.m. to 4 p.m.

Postal application forms in PDF format can be downloaded from the General Register Office website. When filling in your form, if you do not have an exact index entry and reference code, try to provide as much information as possible. Completed application forms, together with the required fee, should be sent to:

General Register Office
PO Box 2
Southport
Merseyside PR8 2JD

Application forms can also be **faxed** to the General Register Office, together with details of your credit or debit card. The fax number is 01704 550 013.

Certificate orders can take from about four days up to around three weeks, depending on demand and staffing levels. If you require a certificate quickly you can request a priority order, which is despatched the next day if ordered before 4 p.m. The cost for this priority service is between £23 and £27.50, depending on how much information you have and how you order the certificate.

If you are not sure whether the index entry is for the exact event that you are looking for, or if you have found more than one possible entry, you can request that the certificate is only issued if it meets certain criteria, which is called **reference checking**. For example, if you are placing an order for a certificate relating to an index entry for the death of Gladys Johnson, you can ask the staff to check first whether she was the widow of Phillip Johnson or if her maiden name was Heywood before they issue the certificate. If these details do not match the certificate will not be issued; instead you will receive a notification and a partial refund.

District register offices can issue certificates from information contained in their original registers. The General Register Office index reference is not necessary when ordering from a local office. Some district register offices have helpful, friendly staff and will issue certificates very quickly. However, some are so busy that they will not issue certificates for the purposes of family history or if you do not know the exact date and place of the event. As a result of boundary changes and merging of districts, the district in which the event took place might also no longer exist.

You can search for a district register office by location or postcode from the home page of the General Register Office website. Alternatively, your local phone book should contain an entry under 'Registration of Births, Deaths and Marriages'.

What Certificates Tell You

Birth certificates give information not just about the child but also about the parents. There are restrictions on order-ing certificates for births registered less than 50 years ago, due to General Register Office anti-fraud measures. If you want to order a birth certificate other than your own and do not know the exact date and place of birth of the per-son concerned, you may be questioned about your reason for applying and asked to show identification.

In the 1970s the format of birth certificates changed from the traditional 'landscape' shape to the more modern 'portrait' shape, with more sections to show additional information.

The date and place of birth of the child are given, as well as the name and occupation of the father (modern certificates also give the occupation of the mother), the mother's maiden name, the name and address of the per-son who registered the birth (usually one or both parents) and the date of registration. New-format certificates also show the place of birth of each parent.

FC 231041

CERTIFIED COPY of an ENTRY
Pursuant to the Births and Deaths Registration Act 1953

				Registration District	Southport				
1967.		Birth in the Sub-district of Southport				in the Metropolitan District of Sefton			
Columns:- 1	2	3	4	5	6	7	8	9	10
No.	When and where born	Name, if any	Sex	Name, and surname of father	Name, surname and maiden surname of mother	Occupation of father	Signature, description, and residence of informant	When registered	Signature of registrar	Name entered after registration
106	Seventh June 1967 General Hospital Southport	Andrew Peter	Boy	Michael Peter Morgan	Helen Morgan Formerly Jones of 60 Market Street Southport	Boilermaker	Helen Morgan Mother 60 Market Street	Twenty-Seventh June 1967	P Wilson Registrar	

Certified to be a true copy of an entry in a register in my custody.

T Wilson   SPECIMEN   Superintendent Registrar

19th September 2006 Date

CAUTION: THERE ARE OFFENCES RELATING TO FALSIFYING OR ALTERING A CERTIFICATE AND USING OR POSSESSING A FALSE CERTIFICATE. ©CROWN COPYRIGHT

WARNING: A CERTIFICATE IS NOT EVIDENCE OF IDENTITY.

Specimen landscape and portrait birth certificates.
© Crown Copyright. Published by permission of HMSO and the Office for National Statistics.

BD 355494

CERTIFIED COPY OF AN ENTRY
Pursuant to the Births and Deaths Registration Act 1953

SPECIMEN

BIRTH   Entry No. 106

Registration district	Southport	Administrative area Metropolitan District of Sefton
Sub-district	Southport	

1. Date and place of birth CHILD
Second September 2006
General Hospital Southport

2. Name and surname
Emily May POTTERTON   3. Sex Female

4. Name and surname FATHER
Kevin Sean POTTERTON

5. Place of birth
Irish Republic   6. Occupation Plumber

7. Name and surname MOTHER
Georgina POTTERTON

8.(a) Place of birth
Preston Lancashire   8.(b) Occupation School Teacher

9.(a) Maiden surname
BRISTOW   9.(b) Surname at marriage if different from maiden surname

10. Usual address (if different from place of child's birth)
68 Furlington Road Southport

11. Name and surname (if not the mother or father) INFORMANT 12. Qualification Mother

13. Usual address (if different from that in 10 above)

14. I certify that the particulars entered above are true to the best of my knowledge and belief
G Potterton   Signature of Informant

15. Date of registration
Twenty First September 2006   16. Signature of registrar P Johns Registrar

17. Name given after registration, and surname

Certified to be a true copy of an entry in a register in my custody.

P. Johns   *Superintendent Registrar *Registrar *Strike out whichever does not apply   Date 21 September 2006

CAUTION: THERE ARE OFFENCES RELATING TO FALSIFYING OR ALTERING A CERTIFICATE AND USING OR POSSESSING A FALSE CERTIFICATE. ©CROWN COPYRIGHT

WARNING: A CERTIFICATE IS NOT EVIDENCE OF IDENTITY.

Barbara's bridesmaid

Wendy had been bridesmaid to her best friend, Barbara Ward, in York in 1968. Barbara had married a local student from outside the area whose first name was Jonathan, but Wendy couldn't remember his surname. She thought that they had moved to the south coast and remembered hearing through a mutual acquaintance that Barbara had a daughter.

Now living in Buckinghamshire, Wendy decided to look for Barbara using General Register Office records, and spent a day at the Family Records Centre searching through indexes.

She found the marriage of Barbara Ward to Jonathan Ellis in the district of York in the indexes for 1968 – this fitted with what Wendy remembered, so she now had Barbara's surname.

She had to search for quite some time for the birth index entry of Barbara's daughter, but eventually located a likely entry in one of the volumes for 1974: Ellis, Jennifer M (mother's maiden name Ward), district of Winchester.

She was sure this was her friend's child. Barbara's mother was called Jennifer, so the daughter must have been named after her grandmother. Both surnames and the districts fitted too. However, Jennifer was born a long time ago and the family may have moved.

Wendy spent some more time searching indexes, this time looking for a marriage for Jennifer – if she found this entry it would give more recent information about the family. Starting in 1992, when Jennifer would have been 18, Wendy discovered that the newer annual indexes were much quicker to search. She found an entry that seemed to fit in the volume for 1997: Ellis, Jennifer M, spouse Wilson, district of Winchester.

With this information and the codes that were included with the index entry, Wendy was able to order Jennifer's marriage certificate. It arrived in the post just over a week later and confirmed that the bride's father was Jonathan, so this was Barbara's daughter. The address that Jennifer provided at the time of her marriage was in Winchester and Wendy decided to write a short letter in the hope that Barbara still lived there.

After two weeks, when she had given up hope, a call came from Barbara, who was delighted to hear from her old friend. Barbara explained that she had been on holiday when the letter arrived, hence the delay in responding. The friends spent hours talking on the phone and eventually met up for a weekend of chat and nostalgia. They are still regularly in touch.

Specimen of a marriage certificate. © Crown Copyright. Published by permission of HMSO and the Office for National Statistics.

A **marriage** certificate gives the full names and ages of both parties, their occupations, usual addresses and the names and occupations of both their fathers.

Close cousins

Graham and Debbie are first cousins: their dads were brothers and when they were growing up both families lived in the same road. Graham and Debbie were great friends as they were both only children – they were more like brother and sister than cousins. Graham looked after Debbie and Debbie looked up to Graham. They attended the same school, played with the same friends, and were always in and out of each other's houses.

When Graham was 14 and Debbie was 11, Debbie's father died suddenly. Debbie's mother was distraught and could not bear to remain living in the same house with so many memories of her husband. She quickly sold up and moved back to Guildford, the town where her parents lived. She remarried soon after, something that Graham's father did not approve of, and the two families gradually lost touch.

Graham approached me at the age of 37 as he was due to get married in a few months. He had thought more and more about Debbie as he got older. Now that his father was suffering from dementia and in a nursing home, he felt that his side of his family would be sadly underrepresented at his wedding. His mother remembered little about Debbie and her mother, so it was up to Graham to try to locate her.

He knew the year that Debbie was born and I was able to find her birth record quite easily. Her birth certificate was obtained, which informed me that her full name was Deborah Veronica Gilchrist and her parents were Donald Gilchrist and Maureen Evaline Gilchrist née Packham. A marriage search for Debbie drew a blank and she did not appear on the electoral register. I then looked for a second marriage for her mother Maureen and found an entry for a marriage of Maureen E Gilchrist to Edmonds in the district of Guildford two years after the death of Debbie's father.

Not finding Maureen Edmonds on the electoral register, I decided to check whether she had died. There was indeed an entry that looked likely and showed that a Maureen Evaline Edmonds (born 7 July 1941) had died in the district of Guildford in June 1998. Graham was sad to hear this, as he had fond memories of his aunt and she had died young. Her death certificate was obtained and showed that her daughter Debbie, now Deborah Veronica Leach, had registered the death. The address that she gave at the time was in Edinburgh. I wrote to this address asking Debbie to contact me because a relative was attempting to get in touch with her.

She responded within days and was delighted to hear that Graham was trying to find her – she had also been looking for him! She explained that she had gone to study in Edinburgh where she met her husband, they married and she had remained in Scotland (the fact that they married in Scotland explained why no marriage record could be found in England and Wales). She had tried writing to Graham and his family at their last known address when her mother became ill with cancer, but did not receive a reply because they had moved.

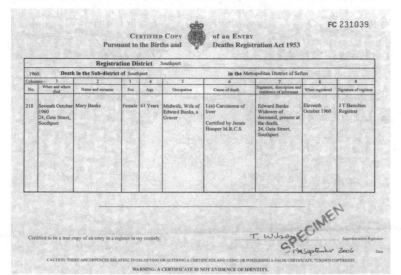

FC 231039

CERTIFIED COPY of an **ENTRY**
Pursuant to the Births and **Deaths Registration Act 1953**

Registration District Southport

1960. **Death in the Sub-district of** Southport   in the Metropolitan District of Sefton

Columns:- 1	2	3	4	5	6	7	8	9
No.	When and where died	Name and surname	Sex	Age	Occupation	Cause of death	Signature, description and residence of informant	When registered	Signature of registrar
218	Seventh October 1960 24, Gate Street, Southport	Mary Banks	Female	61 Years	Midwife, Wife of Edward Banks, a Grocer	I (a) Carcinoma of liver Certified by James Hooper M.R.C.S.	Edward Banks Widower of deceased, present at the death, 24, Gate Street, Southport	Eleventh October 1960	J T Hamilton Registrar

Certified to be a true copy of an entry in a register in my custody.

T. Wilson   *Superintendent Registrar*

SPECIMEN

19th September 2006   Date

CAUTION: THERE ARE OFFENCES RELATING TO FALSIFYING OR ALTERING A CERTIFICATE AND USING OR POSSESSING A FALSE CERTIFICATE. ©CROWN COPYRIGHT

WARNING: A CERTIFICATE IS NOT EVIDENCE OF IDENTITY.

CERTIFIED COPY **OF AN ENTRY**   BW 217650
Pursuant to the Births and **Deaths Registration Act 1953**

DEATH   Entry No. 132

Registration district	Southport	Administrative area Metropolitan District of Sefton
Sub-district	Southport	

1. Date and place of death
Ninth May 2006
General Hospital Southport

2. Name and surname
Abigail WILKINSON

3. Sex   Female

4. Maiden surname of woman who has married   LLOYD

5. Date and place of birth
12th March 1936   Rugby Warwickshire

6. Occupation and usual address
Seamstress (Retired)
Widow of Robert WILKINSON Bricklayer (Retired)
29 Craven Road Southport

7(a) Name and surname of informant
Douglas WILKINSON

(b) Qualification
Son
Present at death

(c) Usual address
86 Pitt Street Southport

8. Cause of death
I (a) Carcinomatosis
(b) Carcinoma of Breast

Certified by B Singh MB

9. I certify that the particulars given by me above are true to the best of my knowledge and belief
D Wilkinson   Signature of informant

10. Date of registration
Eleventh May 2006

11. Signature of registrar
K Thornton Registrar

Certified to be a true copy of an entry in a register in my custody.

K Thornton   *Superintendent Registrar* *Registrar*   Date 11 May 2006

CAUTION: THERE ARE OFFENCES RELATING TO FALSIFYING OR ALTERING A CERTIFICATE AND USING OR POSSESSING A FALSE CERTIFICATE. ©CROWN COPYRIGHT

WARNING: A CERTIFICATE IS NOT EVIDENCE OF IDENTITY.

Specimen landscape and portrait death certificates.
© Crown Copyright.
Published by permission of HMSO and the Office for National Statistics.

Debbie attended Graham's wedding later that year with her husband and young daughter. The cousins caught up with 25 years of news and renewed their previously close relationship. Since then Graham and his new wife have visited Debbie in Scotland. 'I can't thank you enough for finding my "little sister",' said Graham in a letter to me after his trip to Scotland. 'Now that we have found each other we are determined never to lose touch again.'

Modern **death** certificates give more information than the older landscape versions. The most important piece of information that I am usually interested in when ordering a death certificate is the name, relationship and address of the informant – the person, usually a relative, who registered the death.

Records in Other Parts of the British Isles

The records described above only cover events in England and Wales. Other parts of the British Isles have their own records, each with their own system of indexing, ordering and policy on access to information from the registers.

General Register Office for Scotland
www.gro-scotland.gov.uk
New Register House
3 West Register Street
Edinburgh EH1 3YT
Tel: 0131 334 0380

General Register Office for Northern Ireland
www.groni.gov.uk
Oxford House
49/55 Chichester Street
Belfast BT1 4HL
Tel: 028 90 252 000

General Register Office for the Republic of Ireland
www.groireland.ie
Government Offices
Convent Road
Roscommon
Ireland
Tel: +353 (0)90 663 2900

Chapter Six

LOCATING OTHER PUBLIC RECORDS

In addition to records of life events, there are many other records that are available to the public and can help to trace people.

Wills and Probate

When someone makes a will, during their lifetime this remains a confidential document. Once a person has died and the will has been 'proved' (in other words, the estate has been distributed), the will becomes a public document. If a person dies intestate (that is, without leaving a will) and a relative subsequently applies for probate, a grant is issued; this is also public information.

Wills can contain detailed information, not just about the deceased but about the family members who inherit from them (their 'beneficiaries'). Therefore, when looking for a particular individual I will often seek out wills for their parents. The names and relationship to the deceased (and more recently also addresses) of the beneficiaries at the time the will was made can provide details that lead directly to a surviving family member. The names and addresses of executors are also given and, even if they are not related to the deceased, the executors could be approached for information about the family members you are seeking.

Making a will is very important, not just for old people or those who have children, but for everyone. Most of us know this but still put off making a will or add it to a mental 'list of things to do one day when I have time'.

The rules about who inherits money and property if a will isn't made, and who becomes guardian to any minor children, are quite complicated. There have been many legal battles between relatives who thought that they were entitled to inherit and have been disappointed. Making a will ensures that your money and property are passed on to the people of your choice after your death. If you don't make decisions and take action during your lifetime, the matter will be out of your hands and your assets could be inherited by someone you don't like very much or don't even know.

With today's smaller families it is not unusual for someone to die having no close blood relatives. Sometimes cousins who haven't seen the person for years or even who have never been in touch receive an unexpected inheritance (perhaps when stepchildren or close friends were promised that they would be left a share of the estate).

Copies of wills and grants cost £5. They can be obtained by applying in person or by post. You will need the full name of the deceased and the date of death. Applications for wills are not accepted by telephone.

Indexes of wills and copies of wills and grants are available in person to search at:

Principal Probate Registry
www.hmcourts-service.gov.uk (click on 'Wills and
    probate' and then 'Information here')
42-49 High Holborn
London WC1V 6NP

You can also apply at one of the district probate offices throughout the country (see website for details). If you are visiting the Principal Probate Registry or one of the district offices, you can search indexes by name without needing the exact date of death. If you are aware of the approximate time when a person died you can search for any will for a period after the death. Please note that the date that an cntry appears on the index is the date when the will was proved, not the date of death. Complex wills and estates can sometimes take a few years to distribute, so if this might be the case do continue the search beyond the year in which the person died.

Copies of wills and grants by post are issued from:

District Probate Registry
Postal Searches & Copies Dept
York Probate Sub-Registry
1st Floor, Castle Chambers
Clifford Street
York YO1 9RG

An application form for postal applications can be downloaded from the HM Courts Service website, www.hmcourts-service.gov.uk.

Where there's a will...

Warren wanted to find his cousin, Lyndsay, after returning to the UK following 12 years working in Canada. 'I teach engineering,' says Warren, 'and when I was offered a job in Canada I jumped at the chance. Being recently divorced I was keen to escape and make a fresh start. One contract led to another and eventually I was taken on by the college as a permanent member of staff. I kept in touch with my parents, of course, but didn't worry too much about other family members because Mum and Dad could always tell me where they were and keep me updated with news.'

Warren's father died after he had been in Canada for 10 years. At first his mother coped, but she soon started to develop memory problems. She also had a fall and broke her hip, making independent living very difficult. Having become bored with his job and worrying constantly about his mother, Warren decided to take unpaid leave to care for her. 'Being an only child, I felt that it was my responsibility to be there with Mum.'

Adjusting to life back in the UK was difficult for Warren, but he was pleased to catch up with friends. One person he really wanted to see was Lyndsay. She was the daughter of his mother's late brother Bill. When Bill had died 10 years previously, Warren had flown over from Canada for the funeral. This had been the last time he saw Lyndsay. 'We chatted for a long time at the wake,' says Warren, 'reminiscing about the times we had spent together as children. Lyndsay was my only cousin and around the same age, so we had been like brother and sister as kids.'

Warren decided to find Lyndsay, but discovered that it was not as easy as he had hoped. 'I went to the library, joined Friends Reunited and Genes Reunited, fiddled around on the internet for hours and asked everyone I could think of, but Lyndsay was very elusive! In the end, I gave up and called Karen at People Search, because I had run out of ideas and really didn't have the time to do more.'

We made the breakthrough in this case by finding the will of Lyndsay's mother, Sheila. Warren told me that his Uncle Bill and Auntie Sheila had lived in a small Northumberland village. When I looked for Sheila on the electoral register there was no current entry and no evidence from indexes that she had remarried. I checked death records and found an entry four years previously that seemed to match, so I ordered the death certificate. Disappointingly, Sheila's death was not registered by Lyndsay but by an unrelated person, suggesting that Lyndsay had not been available at the time. A search was then made for Sheila's will and luckily, when this arrived, it was quite detailed. The main beneficiary of the will was Lyndsay, with a different surname and an address in the Channel Islands.

Warren wrote to the address and received a call from his excited cousin a few days later. Lyndsay told him how she had moved to Jersey to work in a bank there about seven years previously. She had married a colleague and was now settled in Jersey. 'It has been great,' says Warren. 'We have visited each other and I'm now great friends with Lyndsay's husband Rob. It feels like having a new family.'

For **wills in Scotland**, contact:

> National Archives of Scotland
> www.nas.gov.uk
> HM General Register House
> 2 Princes Street
> Edinburgh EH1 3YY
> Tel: 0131 535 1314
> Email: enquiries@nas.gov.uk

For **wills in Northern Ireland**, contact:

> Probate and Matrimonial Office
> Royal Courts of Justice (Ulster)
> Chichester Street
> Belfast BT1 3JF
> Tel: 028 9023 5111

For **wills in the Republic of Ireland**, contact:

> Probate Office
> Four Courts
> Dublin
> Tel: +353 (0)1 725 555

Divorce

Modern divorce records are never made available to the public. Documents relating to divorce are seen as far too private ever to be read by anyone else. Therefore, very few divorce papers after 1937 are available for public consultation. Some historical divorce records do survive and can be viewed at The National Archives in Kew, London (www.nationalarchives.gov.uk). While these might be very interesting to those researching their family history, they are of little use to someone looking for a living person. Only confirmation that a couple have divorced, in the form of a copy of the decree absolute, can now be obtained.

You will need to know not just the names of both parties but also the date and place of their marriage, so unless you were there and remember this exactly it will be necessary first of all to order a copy of the couple's marriage certificate. I rarely apply for confirmation of a divorce as it is expensive: currently £20 for a 10-year search including a copy of the decree absolute if found.

Copies of decrees absolute can be requested from:

Principal Registry of the Family Division
Decree Absolute Section
First Avenue House
42-49 High Holborn
London WC1V 6NP
Tel: 020 7947 7017

Missing mum

'I haven't seen my mum since I was three years old,' said Rowena when she first called to ask me for help. Rowena's mother, Jeanette, had an affair with a work colleague. When this was discovered, Rowena's dad sent Jeanette packing. He later applied for, and was granted, full custody of his young daughter. 'Dad never remarried but I didn't really feel the loss of my mum that much until I got married and had children myself,' Rowena said. 'I had my aunt and gran, but they were my dad's relatives. My mum was never spoken about and although I sometimes felt a bit out of place at school my dad and I were very close, which helped to compensate.'

After her marriage at the age of 20, Rowena started to think a lot about her mum. When she moved out of the home she shared with her father, she was given a box of documents that included her birth certificate. Hiding at the bottom was a photograph of her parents on their wedding day. 'It was then that it hit me,' she said. 'My own mum, my closest relative, had missed my wedding. I tried to ask Dad some questions about her but met with a brick wall. He was obviously still bitter about the affair and hurt that I even wanted to talk about Mum. He was the abandoned one, after all, and he had been around for me while she had just left me.' Rowena understood her father's distress, but was determined to find her mother, if only to hear her side of the story.

Jeanette was traced and, in order to ensure that her address remained confidential should she wish, I forwarded her a letter from Rowena. Jeanette called me a few days later and asked if she could correspond with Rowena through me. Rowena was delighted with the very long letter. 'It was everything I had hoped for,' she said. 'Mum explained everything to me: how she didn't want to leave me, how angry my dad was, how she had fought to keep me and how she had thought of me every day. I learned that I had a half-sister called Sarah, who lives in Spain, and a nephew called Oliver, which is just great.' There were also photographs of Jeanette and her new husband, Gerry, and Sarah and Oliver. After just two weeks Jeanette and Rowena met for the first time in almost 20 years. A visit to Spain is planned next year.

'Dad still doesn't know,' says Rowena, 'and it is a shame that I can't tell him, but he just wouldn't accept it. I don't have any regrets, though, and I'm looking forward to having my mum and sister in my life from now on.'

The decree absolute will not contain details of addresses at the time of the divorce, it will simply show that two people who married on a certain date are now divorced. From this date you can then perhaps look for a remarriage of the person you are seeking. If another person was involved in the divorce as a third party (where adultery was the reason for the divorce), they might be named as the co-respondent. This often provides a clue to a subsequent marriage. Remember also that these days it is common for women to revert to their maiden name once they are divorced.

Like one of the family

Gillian's son Brian had a best friend called William, to whom he had been very close through their school and college years. Gillian had a soft spot for William because his mother had died when he was young and his father worked long hours, meaning that William spent a lot of time at Gillian's house. 'I was like an honorary mother to William,' she explained, 'and he was one of the family for many years.'

When William married Anna at the age of 19, Gillian and Brian attended the wedding, but soon after this Brian moved away to study in another part of the country. Gillian and Brian independently remained in touch with William and Anna by occasional letter and phone call. However, when Gillian moved house from Surrey to the south coast several years later and wrote to them, the letter was returned marked 'Gone away'.

When Brian was killed in a tragic accident the following year, Gillian was desperate to inform William but did not know how to find him. 'I tried the internet,' she said, 'but his surname is quite common, he doesn't have a middle name, and there didn't seem to be a William and Anna with that surname living at the same address. At this stage I gave up and contacted Karen at People Search for help.' By this time Gillian had decided that, having no other close family and planning on making her will, she would like to leave some of her estate to William. It became even more impor-tant, therefore, that he was located.

I started by trying to discover if William and Anna were still married. They had been very young and there did not seem to have been any children from the marriage recorded in the birth indexes. The search for a divorce resulted in a decree absolute dated six years after the marriage and nam-ing a co-respondent, 'Wendy Ann Edwards'. I then looked at the marriage indexes and found an entry showing that William and Wendy had married within a few months of the divorce. This quickly led me to an electoral register entry on Tracesmart for William and Wendy living together in the Scottish Highlands! A listed phone number was included in the entry and I was sure that William would be pleased to hear from Gillian, so I was happy to give her all of this information.

A few days later I received a call from an excited Gillian. She told me that she and William had talked for hours on the phone and that he and his new wife had invited her to stay with them the following weekend. William was a little embarrassed about his divorce from Anna, so hadn't been in touch to inform Gillian or Brian. When he married Wendy they both wanted a fresh start in a new place so had decided to buy a guest house in Scotland, which was doing well.

The weekend was a great success and now Gillian is in regular contact with the couple.

Records of **divorce in Scotland** up to 1984 are held at the National Archives of Scotland (see page 100 for contact details). Post-1984 records are held at the General Register Office for Scotland (see page 92 for contact details).

Records of **divorce in Northern Ireland** are held at:

Public Record Office for Northern Ireland
www.proni.gov.uk
66 Balmoral Avenue
Belfast BT9 6NY
Tel: 028 9025 5905
Email: proni@dcalni.gov.uk

Records of **divorce in the Republic of Ireland** are only available from the court by which the divorce was granted.

Cemetery, Burial and Obituary Records

These often overlooked records can provide invaluable information about families.

Local authority cemeteries may be able to tell you where someone is buried, who the owner of a grave is and whether there is an inscription. If cremated, the family of the deceased may have placed an entry in a book of remembrance or have arranged a permanent memorial such as a plaque, tree or bench with an inscription.

It can sometimes be difficult to find out where someone was buried or cremated and it can involve phoning around cemeteries and crematoria in the area where the person lived. Sometimes there might be a fee to pay for a grave search and location map.

Yellow Pages has an entry under 'Cemeteries and Crematoria', or search by local authority and cemeteries on the internet to find the website of the council that is responsible for cemeteries in the relevant arca. There are also partial transcriptions of burial records on www.interment.net/uk/index.htm.

Obituaries and death notices can be a mine of information. If someone of note or a local longstanding resident dies, the event may well be reported in the local paper. Death notices can also give clues about family members. Although it is unusual now, in the past it was not uncommon to find long reports of funerals, including lists of the mourners and their relationships to the deceased.

The following is typical of a report in a district newspaper in the early 1950s:

Mrs Winnie Nelson

The funeral took place of local resident Mrs Winnie Nelson on Friday last. She died the previous Thursday at her home in Rose Street after a fall down the stairs. Mrs Nelson, widow of the late Geoffrey Nelson, was the secretary of the local gardening group and was well known for her beautiful dahlias.

The Reverend W Cross spoke of Winnie's devotion to her family and her love of the outdoors. Mourners were led by her sister, Mrs Gladys Toogood, who travelled from Cumbria to bid farewell. Nieces Miss Diane Toogood and Mrs Caroline Pegg were also present as was her nephew, Mr Toby Toogood. Winnie's daughter, Mrs Yvette Collins, was unable to attend as she is heavy with child and could not endure the journey from Exeter where her husband is working at present. Mrs Collins sent a large floral tribute with a note saying 'Mum, I will miss you. Rest in peace, Yve x'.

Pall bearers and other mourners included some of Winnie's fellow gardeners, Mrs P Hicks, Mr R Hatch, Mrs N Goodridge, Mr J Collier, Mrs M Ross and Mrs S Tindall. Winnie was laid to rest with her late husband Geoffrey in the leafy west corner of the church cemetery. Most of the women gathered at the graveside were in a distressed state after the interment.

Mrs Ross, who now takes over as secretary of the gardening club, said that Winnie's allotment is now available for rent and applications, care of the village hall post box, would be welcome.

Land Registry

The Land Registry keeps records of property and land in England and Wales. It is responsible for registering title (ownership) to land and buildings and also records property transactions (sales and mortgages). The Land Registry has undergone changes and modernisation to the way records are kept and in 2002 the massive task of computerising 18 million registered titles was completed. Not all property is registered, but a high percentage of residential property ownership will be recorded.

Read more about the Land Registry by visiting its website, www.landreg.gov.uk.

The title register relating to a particular property will tell you the full names of the registered owners and the date that property ownership was transferred to them. If the property is mortgaged, or has any secured borrowing against the value, the name of the lender and amount of the mortgage or loan will also be recorded.

The quickest and most convenient way to obtain a copy of a title register is from the Land Register Online website, www.landregisteronline.gov.uk. The cost for downloading a copy of a title register is currently £3, payable through a secure server.

Applications can also be made by post for copies of title registers. You can download an application form from the Land Registry website (see above) or call one of the district offices for more information. Land Registry district office contact details are shown on the main website, or look in the alphabetical section of your phone book

Title number: CS72510

This title is dealt with by Land Registry, Plymouth Office.

The following extract contains information taken from the register of the above title number. A full copy of the register accompanies this document and you should read that in order to be sure that these brief details are complete.

Neither this extract nor the full copy is an 'official copy' of the register. An official copy of the register is admissible in evidence in a court to the same extent as the original. A person is entitled to be indemnified by the registrar if he suffers loss by reason of a mistake in an official copy.

This extract shows information current on [date and time] and so does not take account of any application made after that time even if pending in the Land Registry when this extract was issued.

REGISTER EXTRACT

Title Number	: CS72510
Address of Property	: 23 Cottage Lane, Kerwick, PL14 3JP.
Price Paid/Value Stated	: £128,000
Registered Owners	: Peter Andrew Bartram and Susan Helen Bartram of
	: 23 Cottage Lane, Kerwick, (PL14 3JP).
Lender	: ILKINGHAM BUILDING SOCIETY

The title number is Land Registry's unique reference number for this registered land.

The price paid/value stated information has been entered in the register since 1 April 2000. It is based on information contained in the transfer or application form lodged with us. It has not been verified by us and may not represent the full market value of the property.

Specimen register

This is a copy of the register of the title number set out immediately below, showing the entries in the register on [date and time]. This copy does not take account of any application made after that time even if still pending in the Land Registry when this copy was issued.

This copy is not an 'official copy' of the register. An official copy of the register is admissible in evidence in a court to the same extent as the original. A person is entitled to be indemnified by the registrar if he suffers loss by reason of a mistake in an official copy. If you want to obtain an official copy, Land Registry's website (www.landregistry.gov.uk) explains how to do this.

TITLE NUMBER : CS72510   PROPERTY REGISTER

CORNSHIRE : MARADON

1. (29 August 1974) The Freehold land shown edged with red on the plan of the above Title filed at the Registry and being 23 Cottage Lane, Kerwick, (PL14 3JP).

2. (29 August 1974) The land tinted yellow on the title plan has the benefit of the following rights granted by the Conveyance dated 27 July 1968 referred to in the charges register:-

    "TOGETHER WITH the benefit of a right of way on foot only over that part of the shared accessway belonging to 25 Cottage Lane."

3. (29 August 1974) The land has the benefit of the rights granted by the Transfer dated 21 August 1974 referred to in the Charges Register.

END OF PROPERTY REGISTER

The title number is Land Registry's unique reference number for this registered land.

This is the date that the entry was made in the register.

Specimen partial register entry.

under 'Land Registry' for details of your nearest office. Postal applications should be sent to:

> The Customer Information Centre
> Room 105
> The Harrow District Land Registry
> Lyon House, Lyon Road
> Harrow HA1 2EU

For information about **property and land ownership in Scotland**, contact:

> Registers of Scotland Executive Agency
> www.ros.gov.uk
> Edinburgh Customer Service Centre
> Erskine House
> 68 Queen Street
> Edinburgh EH2 4NF
> Tel: 0845 607 0161
> Fax: 0131 200 3932
> Email: customer.services@ros.gov.uk

For information about **property and land ownership in Northern Ireland**, contact:

> Land Registry of Northern Ireland
> Lincoln Building
> 27-45 Great Victoria Street
> Belfast BT2 7AD
> Tel: 028 90 251 515

Contact details for **land registries in the Republic of Ireland** are available from the Property Registration Authority website, www.landregistry.ie.

Electoral Registers

Also known as voters' lists, these are registers of people who are eligible to vote in households within a parliamentary constituency. They are usually arranged geographically within a ward (sub-area of the constituency), then by street, so until quite recently it has not been possible to search registers by name. This changed when records of voters were computerised and converted into searchable formats.

When the registers were first made available to the public on CD and via the internet in the late 1990s, it was a real breakthrough – anyone in the UK could be found via these discs or databases and researchers were saved from hours of trawling through volumes at local libraries. Unfortunately, researchers were not the only ones benefiting from these resources: companies used them to compile mailing and phoning lists, and people used them to find relatives and lost loves who did not want to be found. The awareness dawned among the general public that this information, collected by local authorities as a statutory requirement, was being sold to absolutely anyone, arousing anger and indignation. Now, voters have the right to request that their details are not sold or made available in registers for public consultation, rather like having an unlisted phone number. Although this rule has only been in place for a few years, already around 20 per cent of the population who register to vote have 'opted out' of the public register and details of their address are not made available.

There are several sources for electoral register information available online, including those mentioned in Chapter 3 – Tracesmart (www.tracesmart.co.uk) and 192 (www.192.com) – as well as Eroll (www.eroll.co.uk). The latter charges a minimum registration of under £10 for one month, but you will need to cancel your subscription if you no longer wish to use the service after that. However, none of these sites has information earlier than 2002.

You may question why out-of-date information from **historical electoral registers** can help you to find someone if they moved from an address many years ago. In fact, the little information that is recorded can be extremely useful at times.

For example, if you are looking for someone called Millie Booker who lived at a particular address a couple of decades ago, the historical electoral register might tell you that her first name is Millicent, her middle initial is D and the name of her husband is Timothy W Booker. This confirms not only Millie's name and the spelling, but also her husband's. Finding a couple is much easier than looking for an individual, provided they have stayed together. If both names are found at another, more recent address, you can be sure that you have the right person.

Early historical registers only feature males. Women householders over the age of 30 could vote from 1918, although in 1928 this was lowered to 21 to match the age at which men could vote. The voting age for all adults was lowered to 18 in 1970. The survival and availability of historical registers vary a great deal between different areas of Britain. They are usually kept by libraries or sometimes archive offices locally or regionally. See www.familia.org.uk for the main library that covers the area where your ancestor lived.

Some local authorities have an almost complete set of registers dating back to before 1900; others have just a handful of registers from recent decades. Their policy on access also varies, as local government officers interpret laws on data protection in different ways. Some authorities have an 'open access' policy and are happy to look up entries for households in response to enquiries by telephone, letter or email. Other more cautious (some would say zealous) officers take it upon themselves to interpret the law strictly. They may not only refuse to give information from current registers to members of the public who enquire, but also unilaterally impose the removal of former registers (for up to 50 years) from their public rooms. Some libraries and archives will do short searches for free, but many have introduced charged research, which can vary from £8 to £30 per hour for a member of staff to research your enquiry.

If you are not able to obtain information from registers direct from the local libraries or archives that hold them, it may be necessary to employ the services of a researcher to do this for you. For advice about getting professional help, the Association of Genealogists and Researchers in Archives (AGRA, www.agra.org.uk) and the Association of Professional Genealogists (Apgen, www.apgen.org, an American site but with many UK members), both of which are web portals for genealogists worldwide, may be useful. Alternatively, consult genealogical publications to find advertisements for researchers in the area you are looking.

Friends for life

Brenda Stephenson and Ann Ross had been neighbours and friends at an important time in their lives. They had both recently married when they moved into neighbouring houses and had their first babies – both boys – within a few months of each other. Neither of the women had families nearby to help and both felt a little isolated. They supported, encouraged and comforted each other through the first year of sleepless nights, nappies and crying babies. Their sons became best friends and started nursery school on the same day, by which time Ann had had another baby, this time a girl, and Brenda was expecting her second as well.

The boys were due to start primary school together when Brenda's husband received the news that his workplace was closing down. He was offered another job by his company, but it was in another part of the UK. With a wife and two young children to support, he took the decision to relocate rather than accept a small redundancy package and take the chance that he would find another job locally. Although Brenda was upset she supported her husband's decision. Ann was bereft after Brenda and the family left and her son missed his friend dreadfully for quite some time.

Although they remained in touch, Brenda secretly felt let down and deserted by the one person she had depended on for several years. Although she still had her husband, it was just not the same as having a close female friend to talk to. Brenda's early letters were full of information about her new community and the friends she had found. Ann struggled for some time, but finally made new friends. The communication between Ann and Brenda dwindled to the annual Christmas card until eventually, 12 years after Brenda and family had moved, Ann's card was returned marked 'Gone away'.

Feeling angry that Brenda had not told her she was moving, Ann decided to forget all about their friendship and concentrate on building a life for herself now that both her children were older. She got a job in the local police station, which she did well and enjoyed. Meanwhile, Brenda had moved in a hurry, losing her precious address book in the process, when her mother died suddenly. Her father needed her nearby to help with shopping, cooking and housework, things that his wife had always done. He and Brenda were both grief stricken and depressed and it felt important for them to be together. Brenda rented a house and took her children, on the understanding that her husband would follow as soon as they could sell their house and he could find another job. This never happened. He met someone else and stayed where he was.

Six years after the death of her mother and with her youngest child about to start university, Brenda began thinking again about Ann. She wrote to the old address, but Ann too had moved. She tried directory enquiries and found no listed number under Ann's surname. She made a few phone calls to mutual acquaintances, none of whom had seen Ann for several years. She tried an electoral register website, but there were no entries under 'Ann Ross' in the area where she had lived. Brenda was puzzled and called the local library where she used to live to ask if they could suggest anything to help her find Ann.

A helpful member of staff offered to look at historical electoral registers to see when Ann and her husband, who was called Phil, left their last known address. This search revealed that the couple had moved around four years previously. It also uncovered the fact that Ann's first name was not really Ann, but Patricia! She was recorded as Patricia A Ross and her husband as Phillip W Ross. With this information Brenda was able to go back to the internet and find the couple within minutes, still together – they had moved less than five miles.

Brenda dropped Ann a note the same day and her friend called the following morning. They both squealed with delight, apologised to each other for losing touch, and arranged to meet the following week. They now speak weekly on the phone and each has been to stay with the other. 'The years just fell away as soon as we spoke,' said Brenda. 'Through circumstances, we temporarily lost a very close friendship and now we are back in touch we are determined to remain friends for life.'

Directories

We looked briefly at **phone books** and **directory enquiries** services in Chapter 2. Sometimes information about how names are spelled, exact former addresses and old telephone numbers can be useful in a search. Main libraries within local authority areas usually collect and keep old local telephone directories. Look in the current phone book or search online using Yell (www.yell.com) for details of the libraries close to where the person you are seeking used to live.

Alternatively, you could make a visit to the BT archives in London. It holds hundreds of historical telephone directories from all over the UK. It is open to the public by appointment only. Contact:

BT Group Archives
Third Floor
Holborn Telephone Exchange
268–270 High Holborn
London WC1V 7EE
Tel: 020 7440 4220
Fax: 020 7242 1967
Email: archives@bt.com

Ancestry is undertaking a project to index British phone books at the BT archives from 1880 to 1984 and make them available on its site. The first phase, covering London and the Home Counties, is already available, with work well under way to complete all areas and dates. Visit the Ancestry website (www.ancestry.co.uk) for more details.

Once an invaluable resource for researchers everywhere, **street directories** ceased to be published in the 1970s when they became unprofitable. Directories were produced by companies such as Kelly's for each city, county or local community area throughout the country. They listed local residents alphabetically by name, giving their address, and also had a section arranged by street and listing all the people who lived there. The entries were limited to one person per household, usually the 'head' (the man) or sometimes the main resident or property owner. Entries from these directories can help to confirm exact addresses or establish how long a person remained resident at a particular property.

Many local and county or main city libraries have comprehensive runs of old street directories. For details of libraries, see Yellow Pages or your local phone book. Alternatively, visit www.familia.org.uk to find details of libraries that hold the kinds of records you need in the area where you want to research.

Chapter Seven

FINDING PEOPLE THROUGH THEIR WORK AND HOBBIES

An alternative to locating someone at their residential address can be to find them through the work that they do or the activities and interests that they engage in. If the area where the person lives is not known or their name is fairly common, it can seem impossible to narrow down dozens of entries on the electoral register. Finding out about an occupation or hobby can help you eventually to identify the right person.

Directory of British Associations

On my regular visits to the local library, one of the books I consult most often is the *Directory of British Associations* (DBA). This is published by CBD Research (see www.cbdresearch.com/DBA.htm), a company that produces directories and reference books. It is the most wonderfully comprehensive collection of the details of societies, associations and organisations in the UK. Names, addresses, web addresses and contact details of professional, sporting, health, charitable and hobby organisations are listed alphabetically by name, and in addition there is a subject index, making it easy to find an association by type.

Membership of these associations can range from a handful of people with a common interest to thousands of

British Association of Turnip Growers 1962
Hobbs Farm, Clampett, ROOTBRIDGE, Westshire, MZ10 7JH. (chmn/p)
01112 542235   fax 01112 542236
email info@batg.org.uk
http://www.batg.org.uk
Chmn: W B Beatle
▲ Un-incorporated Society
Υ *H; for professional & amateur turnip growers in the UK
Gp Amateur; Professional; Junior (16 & under)
⊗ Conf - Mtgs - Exhib - Comp - Stat - Inf - VE
< Turnip Growers Worldwide
M 200 i, 5 f, 8 org, UK / 9 i, o'seas
¶ Turnip Times (Jnl) – 6; ftm, £12 nm.
Turnippers (for juniors) – 6; ftm, £6 nm.   LM; free.

KEY
chmn/p: Chairman's private address

▲ Legal status

Υ *H; Area of interest is horticultural

Gp Groups

⊗ Activities:
Comp: Competitions
Conf: Conferences
Exhib: Exhibitions & Shows
Inf: Information service available
Mtgs: Regular Meetings
Stat: Collection of Statistics
VE: Visits & Excursions

< Affiliated to

M i: Individuals
f: Firms
o: Organisations

¶ Jnl – 6: Journal produced 6 times per year
ftm: free to members
nm: non-members
LM: List of members

A sample entry from the *Directory of British Associations.*

© CBD Research Ltd.

members within a particular field or profession. Some organisations publish a membership list, others may give details of members on their website. Most, however, have a private membership list that they do not make available to non-members.

Due to data protection legislation they will not be able to give out any personal or contact information about their members. Most, however, may be willing to confirm if someone is a member and forward a pre-stamped letter to the address that they hold for that person. An initial approach may be made to the organisation by phone, letter or email. Whatever method you decide, be polite, offer to cover expenses, and make it clear that you do not expect the organisation to give you any information about the person you are seeking.

Finding Someone Through Their Work

The occupation or profession of the person you are seeking may be an important clue that can help you to find them. Sometimes this information is so valuable that a search is not only quick but also potentially inexpensive.

In the UK many professions such as medicine, law, teaching and architecture are **regulated professions**. This means that it is against the law to practise without being registered and to work or trade within these professions people need to meet the standards of the body in charge. If the person you would like to contact works in a regulated profession, this may be an easy way to find them.

Many regulated professions have printed or online directories of members that may provide a workplace address and phone number. One good example is the register of the Financial Services Authority (FSA). Anyone who offers financial advice on investments, savings or pensions must be registered with the FSA. Its comprehensive, searchable website can be found at www.fsa.gov.uk; click 'FSA Register' and 'Access the FSA Register', then select 'Individuals Search'.

In addition to the more obvious regulated professions, there are dozens of other jobs that people do where they need to be registered, including marine engineer, speech therapist, air traffic controller, forester, meteorologist, surveyor, farrier, driving instructor and London cab driver.

For a comprehensive list of regulated professions, with links to the websites of the professional bodies, visit www.dfes.gov.uk/europeopen/eutouk/authorities_list.shtml or go to www.dfes.gov.uk and enter 'regulated professions' in the search box.

Hundreds of trades and professions, even if they are not regulated, have established and structured **associations** for their members. Librarians, reflexologists, taxidermists and photographers, for example, all have trade associations.

Many of these associations produce a directory of members or have a website that lists them. Try a Google search combining the name of the trade and the words 'association' or 'society'. Alternatively, contact or visit your nearest central library to find out if it has a collection of trade directories.

Family feud

Di wanted to know what had happened to her uncle Derek. There had been a family feud when Di was a teenager; Derek was never mentioned again and, when Di asked about him, her questions were met with silence or a rapid change of subject.

But Di had been close to her uncle, who had read her stories as a child, taken her to the park and bought her ice creams. She did not want to forget him. Her application contained information that I was fairly sure would make this search an easy one: 'occupation: funeral director'. A few minutes on the internet found the professional association for this trade. A call to its office was very productive. Although the staff could not tell me Derek's address, they informed me that Derek was a retired member of the organisation. They agreed to forward a letter to him, which was sent the next day. Within a week Derek had contacted Di and they made plans to meet.

Di discovered that the rift was over his choice of girlfriend more than 35 years before. 'My mother didn't think she was suitable,' he told her. Di was delighted to be in touch with Derek and was soon getting to know his wife, the same woman that Derek's mother had considered 'unsuitable'.

Di called me a few weeks later to tell me that she had no regrets and was enjoying spending time with her new relatives. 'I was not going to let my family stop me from finding Uncle Derek,' she said. 'Knowing my family as I do, and now that I have seen what a lovely lady his wife is, I am sure he made the right choice!'

Company directors in the UK are required by law to disclose personal information to Companies House. When a limited company is registered or a new director appointed, they must provide their full name, date of birth and permanent residential address. These details are made available to the public so that they can make informed choices about a company they may wish to invest in or trade with. Although some company directors object to what they regard as personal information being public, they are offered 'limited liability' in return. This means that they are not held personally responsible for the debts of their company.

To find out from Companies House if someone is a director, you will need to visit one of its offices (see below) or write to the head office in Cardiff giving the person's name and date of birth. This service is not currently available by telephone. Once directorship has been confirmed, you will be told how to apply for a report that gives information about the director, including their address and the names of the companies of which they are a director.

General enquiries
Tel: 0870 333 3636
www.companies-house.gov.uk

Main Office
Companies House
Crown Way
Maindy
Cardiff CF14 3UZ

Edinburgh Office
Companies House
37 Castle Terrace
Edinburgh EH1 2EB

London Office
Companies House Executive Agency
21 Bloomsbury Street
London WC1B 3XD

Information about company directors, including their residential addresses, can also be found on several internet sites. Tracesmart (www.tracesmart.co.uk) includes company director information within its basic searches and results, making this an economical option (see Chapter 3 for more on Tracesmart).

If you just want to find out if someone is a company director, the Duport website has the facility to check by full name and date of birth, but you need to purchase a director report to find out what their residential address is and the names of the companies they hold directorships for. Go to www.duport.co.uk, click on 'Credit Reports', then fill in the name of the person you are seeking under 'Find a UK Director Report'.

Quarrelling over Kathy
Throughout university Don and Mick had been inseparable. They had neighbouring rooms, the same tastes and they hit it off straight away. 'The first night we were there on our own,' says Don, 'was really quite daunting. The parents had

all disappeared and there were a load of bewildered teenagers just hanging around with no one to talk to. Mick was friendly and asked if I wanted to go for a curry – we both love curry! For the next three years we did everything together: studying, sport, socialising. We also encouraged and consoled each other through a string of relationships with girls. In our last term we met a lovely girl called Kathy at the student sports club. We both fell for her pretty quickly, but she was obviously more attracted to Mick than me.

'They started going out together and I was crazy with jealousy. I messed up one of my exams after a fight with Mick and never spoke to him again. I felt resentful towards him for years after, convinced that he was to blame because I didn't get a first. He had ruined my life and I would hate him for ever. I didn't know where he was going or what he was planning to do after uni and I didn't care.

'After a couple of years, however, I started to think about him and miss all the good times we had together. I tried to find a phone number for his parents, but couldn't remember exactly where they lived. I checked the alumni but he wasn't registered and I asked around some mutual acquaintances. One person said that they thought he had gone abroad to do voluntary work and at that stage I resigned myself to never seeing him again.'

Nine years later, married and with a baby son and a successful career in teaching, Don decided to try once more. 'The internet had come along and I hoped it would make things much easier this time. The first time I tried I got nowhere: I put Mick's name into a search engine and received over 1,000 matches. I tried electoral registers, but there were loads of entries and I had no way of telling which one was him. A few days later something that Mick had said years before suddenly came back to me. He had told me that he was going to finish uni, travel for a while, then come back and set up his own company. He joked about how rich he would be, how many cars he would buy and that women would be falling over themselves to marry him.

'I decided to see if he was a registered company director and found the Duport site through Google. I entered his name and there were just six matches, all with dates of birth. I was able to identify Mick easily because he was my age and I remembered his birthday. I ordered his report, costing less than £10, and found that he was director of an electrical engineering company in South London. I called him at work the next day, but when I was put through and he answered I got scared and hung up!

'I decided then that I would go to his workplace and surprise him, so the following week I took the train to London and arrived in his office just before lunchtime. He was called out to see his unexpected visitor and I could see immediately that he was really happy and excited – he gave me a big bear hug! He cancelled all his appointments for the rest of the day and took me to his club for a very long lunch. We didn't stop talking for the next five hours. We both apologised for falling out with each other and agreed that Kathy, whom neither of us had seen since uni, really wasn't worth it.

'We had both missed and thought of each other a great deal in the years that we had been apart. I told him about my wife and son, my postgraduate teacher training and my current job as a department head in a community school. His life since university had been eventful: he had met another volunteer in Africa, they had returned to the UK and married in Gretna Green within seven months. His wife's family was very rich and they had enjoyed a comfortable life with their two daughters.

'The marriage did not last more than five years, but Mick received a financial settlement from his wife that he used to set up his now very successful company. He sees his daughters regularly and has a girlfriend called Jenny. We have since met up as a foursome several times and are planning to take a holiday together next year. I'm just so glad that I made the effort to find Mick and would recommend that anyone wanting to find an old friend does the same, even if they previously parted on bad terms.'

Finding Someone Through Their Hobby

Hobbies and sports in the UK tend to be well structured, with a national association and perhaps regional or county branches. Most also have websites that explain the structure, with contact details for the head office, secretary or local organisers. Although hobby and sport associations may not produce directories of members or list individuals on their websites, you may find someone's name mentioned in online minutes as a committee member, coach or competition winner.

If you don't find a particular individual by searching, there may be another way to make contact. You can write, call or email the secretary or one of the officials to confirm whether the person you are seeking is a member. If they are, ask if the association would be prepared to forward a letter or email to them.

You can find societies and associations for a wide range of sports and hobbies in the *Directory of British Associations* (details at the beginning of this chapter) or by using appropriate search terms online. For example, 'Badminton + National + Association' will immediately find Badminton England, the national association for the sport. Officials, managers, coaches and high-level players may be mentioned on the site and details are held at the head office in Milton Keynes. To find coaches, club secretaries, county and league players, try searching under 'Badminton + Hampshire', for instance.

Getting on swimmingly

Joanne and Cathy had worked together for four years during their early 20s and become close friends. When Cathy married, Joanne helped to organise the wedding and was a witness at the ceremony. One year later Cathy left their workplace to have her first baby, a girl called Megan, and decided to become a stay-at-home mother. Joanne, very much a career girl, became a little tired of 'baby talk' after a while. She was ambitious and quickly gained promotion, which meant moving to another part of the country.

After a few years, contact had dwindled to the annual Christmas card and Joanne barely gave it a thought when this ceased after another promotion and another move. 'I was quite selfish and very focused on my career at that time,' explained Joanne. 'I thought Cathy had become a bit boring.' At the age of 31 something unexpected happened to Joanne: she fell in love. Martin worked in the same office as her and was six years younger. There was talk of marriage and both agreed that they did not want children.

However, Joanne became pregnant when they had been dating for only eight months. Martin was horrified: he said he was too young to be tied down with a family. 'I was devastated,' said Joanne. 'I thought Martin loved me and he ran a mile when he found out about the baby.' Joanne decided to keep her baby, move back to her home town to be near her mother and find a job after the child was born. Baby Daniel came along and Joanne was besotted. She wanted to spend every minute with her son and couldn't bear the thought of leaving him every day to go to work. However, she missed adult company and only saw her mother two or three times a week.

'I started to feel very lonely and isolated,' she said, 'and I missed the workplace social life.' Her thoughts turned to Cathy, who had only lived 30 miles away, so she decided to find her. She dug out her address book and all her old letters and Christmas cards from Cathy. The phone number no longer belonged to Cathy's address as it had been reassigned. Joanne took a drive to the last address she had for Cathy, but she no longer lived there. Reading through the letters, the last one contained information about Megan, Cathy's daughter. At the age of just 7, having had lessons since she was 3, Megan was training hard at swimming and hoping to compete at a high level within a couple of years.

Armed with this information, Joanne went on to the internet and entered the following search terms: 'Megan Ross + swimming'. She scrolled through the results, finding several mentions of Megan competing in regional and national competitions. This led to the website of the swimming club that Megan belonged to and, reading through the list of officials, she found that Cathy was treasurer of her daughter's club. There was an email link, so Joanne sent a short message just saying 'Hello', with brief details about Daniel and news of where she was living.

'I was a bit nervous because I had neglected the friendship, but I needn't have worried,' said Joanne. 'I got a really friendly reply from Cathy the next day and she invited Daniel and me to have lunch with her and her four children!

'Cathy had always wanted a big family and her youngest, a son called Callum, was less than a year older than Daniel. We talked for hours, the boys crawled around happily together, and we have seen each other every couple of weeks since then. I'm so happy that I decided to find Cathy again. Circumstances and differences kept us apart for too long, but fundamentally the strong friendship was still there.'

Chapter Eight

USING AGENCIES AND ORGANISATIONS

Maybe you don't have the time or inclination to do a search yourself. Perhaps you have tried some of the ideas in earlier chapters of this book without success. If you are stuck or just want someone to do the search for you, where do you start?

There are a number of agencies and organisations that help people to find others: some are private, some not for profit or charitable. Choosing the right one for you depends on your relationship to the person you are seeking, the amount of information you have and your budget.

Not-For-Profit Agencies

National Missing Persons Helpline (www.missing persons.org) is a charity established in 1992 to advise and support missing people and those who are left behind. The priority of this charity is the vulnerable who are missing; that is, the elderly, very young, sick or distressed. The Home Office estimates that around 210,000 people are reported missing in the UK each year. Many are found or return within 72 hours, but thousands don't, causing extreme distress to their families and friends.

If a relative is missing without contact and could be considered vulnerable, call the National Missing Persons

Helpline on 0500 700 700 to see if they might be able to help, or least offer some support. They will not always be able to reunite you with the person you are seeking, particularly if that person is an adult of sound mind, but they may try to locate them and find out if they are alive and well.

You might consider an application to **Traceline**, a not-for-profit government letter-forwarding service (note that this is *not* the same as www.traceline.co.uk, which is a commercial company). The advantage this service has is that it has access to confidential government records, including the NHS register. Therefore, if someone is registered with a GP in England and Wales, their current address can be found. The service is also relatively cheap (around £60) and accurate. Provided you are able to supply enough information to identify a particular individual (full name and date of birth at least), you can be sure that the service will locate the correct person, as long as they are resident in England or Wales.

The disadvantages of Traceline are:

* It takes time, sometimes months.
* The service simply forwards a letter from you, it doesn't tell you the address of the person or anything else about them.
* If you get no reply to your letter there is little you can do.
* There are restrictions. For example, Traceline cannot help with adoption-related searches, searches for current or former spouses, or 'in circumstances where contact may prove disruptive'.

See www.gro.gov.uk/gro/content/research/traceline/index.asp for more information. Contact Traceline on 0151 471 4811 or write to:

Traceline
PO Box 106
Southport
PR8 2WA

Established over 100 years ago, the **Salvation Army Family Tracing Service** has operated successfully despite a small number of staff and the many thousands of enquiries it receives each year. It too has a high success rate, but the process can be slow.

The criteria, restrictions and contact procedure are similar to those of Traceline (see above). The Salvation Army will not search for 'alleged fathers' where a child was born within a 'non-marital relationship', so if your parents were not married it is unlikely that it will help.

Contact the Salvation Army Family Tracing Service in London or Belfast for more information, or to request an application form. Its website is www.salvationarmy.org.uk (follow the link to Family Tracing near the bottom of the home page).

The addresses are:

101 Newington Causeway
London SE1 6BN
Tel: 0207 367 4747
(for Great Britain)

4 Curtis Street
Belfast
Tel: 01232 324 730
(for Northern Ireland)

Patricia's is a typical example of a Family Tracing Service success story.

Because life's too short

Patricia, 46, a school supervisor from Derby, and her brother Michael, 43, from Preston, Lancashire, didn't speak for 10 years after an argument about money. Patricia explains:

'Michael and I were the youngest of 10 children and always got on well. When I separated from my first husband and needed somewhere to live, it seemed the perfect solution to move in with Michael. We lived together for a year, but then he moved from Derby to Stoke to live with his partner. He gave me no warning and I was left to pay all the rent by myself. He kept saying he would send me the money, but it never arrived. I was so annoyed that I sold some of the stuff he'd left behind. He wasn't very pleased, and then we stopped speaking to one another. When Michael moved again, we lost touch completely.

'I'd think about him from time to time, but after one failed attempt at finding him through an advert in a magazine, I didn't do anything else about it until 2000. That's when someone told me about trying The Salvation Army's Family Tracing Service. Six weeks after I contacted them, they said they had found Michael and suggested I write him a letter. I wrote: "Dear Mike, I really miss you and want my brother back. Everything that happened is all water under the bridge now. Let's forget it and get in touch. Life's too short to fight."

'He rang me as soon as he got the letter. It felt so strange to be talking to him again after all that time, but he agreed to come over to Derby to meet up. We didn't really talk about what had sparked the whole thing off – it was all in the past, and there didn't seem any point in dwelling on what had happened. Now we are closer than ever, and it feels as if we've never been apart. At the moment, we're just taking each day as it comes and doing our best to make up for missing 10 years of each other's lives.'

Previously published in *Family Matters* newsletter and reproduced with the permission of the Salvation Army Family Tracing Service.

Adoption Agencies

Informal and private adoption has taken place for centuries and references to adoption can be found in records throughout the ages. The legal process of adoption was introduced in England and Wales by the Adoption of Children Act 1926. Successive legislation making significant changes was introduced in 1975 and 1989. Most recently, the Adoption and Children Act 2002 came fully into force on 30 December 2005. This act has implications for those searching for adopted people and also adoptees who want to find their natural family.

Adopted people have two birth records. The first, their original birth certificate, gives details of their name at birth, place of birth and natural mother (and also their natural father, if this was recorded). These records are indexed within the normal General Register Office index of births, and certificates can be ordered without restriction if you know the person's original name and date of birth (except if it is your own certificate and you were adopted before 1975, in which case you will need to see a counsellor before you can be given any information). Only the adoptee can apply for their birth records, so if you know that someone was adopted but do not know the name they were born with, you cannot obtain a copy of their birth certificate.

Once someone has been adopted, a new birth record is issued giving the child's new name and the name of the adoptive parents. A copy of this can be obtained in the same way as for any birth certificate.

Indexes of adopted children are kept at the Family Records Centre. They are arranged alphabetically by adopted surname in annual volumes. No indication is given of the date of birth, district of birth or original name. A copy of the full adoption certificate, showing details such as the date of the adoption, can be obtained from the General Register Office in the same way as a birth certificate, as long as you know the full name of the person after adoption, their date of birth and the full name(s) of the adoptive parent(s).

If your search is adoption related in any way, it is very important for you to have at least one counselling interview with an adoption professional and preferably receive ongoing support before, during and after the search. Adoption reunion is inevitably an emotional process with no guarantee of a happy outcome. Speaking to someone with experience and knowledge of adoption matters will help you to air your expectations and fears, manage your feelings when an approach is made, and support you and your natural relative throughout the process of reunion. Adoption professionals can also advise and assist with tracing your relative or refer you to an agency or researcher who can help you with this.

Read more about adoption history, records and services on the website of the British Association for Adoption and Fostering: www.baaf.org.uk.

If you were adopted, the first step in finding your natural family is to apply for a copy of your original birth certificate and any records relating to your adoption. You can do this by contacting the **Adoptions Section of the General Register Office**:

Room C201
General Register Office
Trafalgar Road
Southport PR8 2HH
Tel: 0151 471 4830 (9 a.m. to 5 p.m. Monday to Friday)
Email: adoptions@ons.gsi.gov.uk

Staff can also check the **Adoption Contact Register** at the General Register Office (www.gro.gov.uk/gro/content/adoptions/adoptioncontactregister) in case any of your birth relatives has left contact details, to be given to you in the event that you try to find them via the register.

If you prefer to speak with someone locally or want to find out what records exist in the area where you were adopted, contact the local authority **social services**. Ask for 'Post-adoption' to speak with someone who will be familiar with post-adoption procedures and local records.

You have a right to access to your birth records (and to certain information from your adoption file if it still exists), but if you were adopted before 12 November 1975 you must have an interview with a trained counsellor first. Once you have obtained your records, when you are ready you may wish to seek help in the form of research information, intermediary services and group or individual support.

Success in the end

Will was adopted at six months and had a happy childhood. Now married with two daughters, he decided to trace his natural mother. He contacted his local social services department, who arranged a meeting to tell him more about the circumstances of his adoption and to talk through the search process.

Will learned that at the time of his birth in the 1960s his mother, Irene, was a young Irish girl, living in London with her brother. Terrified that her parents would find out, her brother helped to keep the pregnancy secret and the baby was quickly adopted.

With the help of an agency, Will discovered that Irene was now married with four other children. The agency also found a current address for Irene's brother. After discussions with his adoption worker, Will decided that to protect his mother the initial approach should be to her brother. A brief letter was sent from the agency asking him to pass a message to Irene.

A very nervous Irene called the agency a few days later – she was in turmoil. Apart from her brother, nobody knew about this child; she feared that her husband would be hurt and angry. Her only message to Will was that, regretfully, she was unable to meet up or have contact with him. This message was conveyed to Will who, although disappointed, tried to be philosophical.

Within two weeks, however, Irene called the agency again. She wanted to know more about Will and was told that he was married with two daughters. She asked the agency to give Will a message: 'I am pleased that you found me. I wish I could see you but at the moment I can't – I hope you understand. I send love and good wishes to you and your family.'

Will was delighted with this and remained hopeful that one day they would meet. Irene continued to call the agency periodically. She reported that she could not stop thinking about her son, her marriage was suffering due to the strain of keeping this secret, and she was attending counselling with a charity that the agency had recommended, which was helping.

Eventually, five months after the initial contact was made, a much calmer Irene called the agency to ask for Will's contact details. With the help of her counsellor, she had found the courage to tell her family about Will. They were surprised but understanding and encouraged Irene to meet with him. The meeting was a success and the two families have now been introduced.

Norcap is an organisation that supports adults affected by adoption:

Norcap
www.norcap.org.uk
112 Church Road
Wheatley
Oxfordshire OX33 1LU
Tel: 01865 875 000

The **Post-Adoption Centre** also provides independent advice, counselling and support to anyone affected by or dealing with the challenges and opportunities of adoption:

Post-Adoption Centre
www.postadoptioncentre.org.uk
5 Torriano Mews
Torriano Avenue
London NW5 2RZ
Tel: 020 7284 0555
Advice line: 0870 777 2197
Email: advice@postadoptioncentre.org.uk

After Adoption is another service that helps anyone affected by adoption:

After Adoption
www.afteradoption.org.uk
Canterbury House
12–14 Chapel Street
Manchester M3 7NH
Tel: 0161 839 4932
Action line: 0800 0568 578

In addition to all the above adoption charities, there are also some **private adoption agencies** that offer search and intermediary services. Although they may be quicker at finding birth relatives, they will inevitably be more expensive. Ensure that any private service you approach is a registered Adoption Support Agency before commissioning it to undertake a search for you.

Adoption records and procedures are different in Scotland to those in England and Wales. Contact **Birthlink**, Scotland's service for people separated by adoption, for more information:

Birthlink
www.birthlink.org.uk
21 Castle Street
Edinburgh EH2 3DN
Tel: 0131 225 6441

For information about adoption records in Northern Ireland, contact the General Register Office (Northern Ireland): www.groni.gov.uk (see Chapter 5 for further contact information).

For information about adoption records in the Republic of Ireland, contact the **Adopted People's Association**:

Adopted People's Association
www.adoptionireland.com
14 Exchequer Street
Dublin 2
Ireland

Tel: +353 (0)1 679 0011 (Mondays and Thursdays,
    2 p.m. to 4 p.m.)
Email: info@adoptionireland.com

Private Research and Investigation Agencies

If it seems that you have tried everything or you've become weary of the search, hiring someone to continue the work for you can be a tempting option. If you decide to do this, be sure to tell the researcher everything you have tried already and supply copies of any documents you have obtained. This saves duplication of work, which may cut the length of time your case takes and the cost. Before considering a private investigator, detective or researcher, do make enquiries with the not-for-profit organisations first, as they have been successful in reuniting countless individuals and will be cheaper than a private researcher or investigator.

Many **genealogists and family researchers** are able to use the same techniques and records that have helped them to trace ancestors to work forward in time and find living persons. Family history magazines carry pages of advertisements from researchers offering their services. How can you choose someone suitable? Read through the adverts to see if any specifically mention tracing living relatives. A telephone call or email enquiring about experience and previous success with this type of search may narrow down your list, as will checking out websites if their addresses are given.

If someone is a member of the Association of Genealogists and Researchers in Archives and displays the

AGRA logo, they have been assessed by the association and work to a code of practice. A directory of members is available online at www.agra.org.uk. For more information send an SAE or for a printed membership list send £2.50 to:

The Secretary
The Association of Genealogists and Researchers in
    Archives
29 Badgers Close
Horsham
West Sussex RH12 5RU

For professional researchers in Scotland, try:

Association of Scottish Genealogists and Researchers in
    Archives
www.asgra.co.uk
93 Colinton Road
Edinburgh EH10 5DF
Tel: 0131 313 1104

For professional researchers in Northern Ireland, contact:

Association of Ulster Genealogists and Record Agents
www.augra.com
Glen Cottage
Glenmachan Road
Belfast BT4 2NP
Email: secretary@augra.com

The organisation for professional researchers in the Republic of Ireland is:

Association of Professional Genealogists in Ireland
www.apgi.ie

Many **investigators** are former police officers or have a legal background. They rarely specialise in tracing, but offer a range of services including surveillance, credit reporting and process serving. Although some of the resources used are the same as for genealogists, investigators tend to rely more on database information, contacts and personal enquiries. They may have access to specialist databases that are not available to the public and this might mean that they are able to locate someone more quickly. They are, however, likely to be more expensive. Discuss fees in detail and set a budget before you agree to hand over your search. You may need to pay a deposit, sign a contact or consent to a minimum fee.

You can find investigators under 'Detective Agencies' in Yellow Pages or at www.yell.com.

There are two main organisations for investigators in the UK:

Association of British Investigators (ABI)
www.theabi.org.uk
10 Bonner Hill
Kingston-upon-Thames
London KT1 3EP
Tel: 0871 474 0006

Institute of Professional Investigators (IPI)
www.ipi.org.uk
Burkhill Business Centre
Provident House
Burrell Row
High Street
Beckenham
Kent BR3 1AT
Tel: 0208 249 6605

Running away

19-year-old Ash was about to start university when he went out one morning and didn't come home. He called his mother a couple of days later, just for long enough to say that he was OK and tell her not to worry. Since then his parents had heard nothing. They discovered that Ash's girlfriend, Sunita, was also missing from her family home. Sunita's parents were distraught and angry, blaming Ash for taking their daughter away. They received one short note from Sunita explaining that she needed to live away from her parents for a while.

The police were contacted by both families but, as both Ash and Sunita were adults and had been in touch with their parents, there was little that they could do. Ash's father, Niraj, called a local investigator in desperation, five months after Ash had left home. 'He was brilliant,' said Niraj. 'He came to my home, talked through everything with me, took some information and photographs of Ash, then promised he would do all he could to find our son.' Niraj paid a deposit and signed a contract, but money did not matter as the family could afford it and Ash's wellbeing was the most important factor.

Less than a month later the call came that Niraj had been waiting for – Ash and Sunita had been found. 'We were overjoyed and wanted to know right away where our son was living,' he said, 'but the investigator was cautious and said that he would visit them first and speak to Ash personally. I can understand that he thought we might be heavy-handed with our son and perhaps force him to come home against his will. We would not have done this, but I can see why he wanted to handle things that way.'

Ash was not surprisingly a little afraid when the investigator arrived at the flat that he shared with Sunita. Eventually, however, after some reassurance, Ash let the investigator in and started to talk. He explained that Sunita was pregnant – the baby was due very soon – and the young couple were very scared of their families. It was shameful to have a child if you were not married, explained Ash, and Sunita's parents were very conventional. They did not approve of Ash and had wanted Sunita to settle down and marry a more traditional boy. They had tried to stop Sunita from seeing Ash and, when the pregnancy was discovered, the young couple decided that getting away from their families was the safest thing for them to do.

The investigator reassured Ash that his father would not be angry. Ash's family missed him very much and just wanted him to be happy. A call was made from the investigator's mobile phone and a long, emotional conversation followed. Ash learned that his older sister was getting married, his grandfather had died and his father had started to

suffer from angina. Ash felt responsible for his father's illness and wondered if the stress of him going missing was
to blame. Nevertheless, both his parents made him feel that
he was loved, missed and not blamed for anything at all.
'We were just so happy to speak to our son,' said Niraj, 'and
we all cried together. We heard about the baby and we were
a bit shocked, but were really just concerned that they were
both OK.'

Niraj and his wife wanted to visit Ash and Sunita as
soon as possible, but they had moved rather a long way.
Also, Sunita was very cautious and she did not want her
family to know where she was living, because she was afraid
that her father and brothers would come and force her to
return to the family home. After a few more phone calls, the
birth of a baby daughter and reassurance that Sunita's family would not be told, Ash agreed that his parents could visit
them. 'It was a very emotional day,' said Niraj. 'We drove for
many hours and arrived at the place where our son was living. It was very small and shabby, they obviously didn't have
very much money, and Ash was working long hours in a café
to support Sunita and the baby.'

Niraj and his wife were able to provide some immediate
financial assistance, which enabled Ash and Sunita to buy
things for the baby. It also helped Ash to reduce his long
working hours and think about returning to his studies.
'Calling that investigator was the best thing I could have
done,' says Niraj, 'and I'm so grateful to him for bringing
our son back to his family.'

Chapter Nine

FINDING PEOPLE WORLDWIDE

The number of people emigrating from the UK has been rising for a number of years, as living abroad has become increasingly popular. In 1971 240,000 British people were recorded as permanently leaving the UK. By 2004 the number had risen to just under 340,000. According to recent Foreign and Commonwealth Office statistics, around 4.5 million Britons are now living overseas.

When someone has left the UK it can seem a daunting task to locate them, particularly if you don't know which country they have settled in. I usually start a search for a person living abroad by obtaining a copy of their birth certificate (see Chapter 5) to confirm their full name and date of birth – you may need this if preliminary searches don't find them.

Contacts in the UK

If it is likely that the person has relatives still living in the UK, it will almost certainly be quicker and cheaper to locate them and ask for contact details or if they can forward a message. I have successfully located people by using this approach on many occasions. If you know the names of the person's parents, siblings or children, try a search for them first using one of the electoral register sites (see Chapter 3). If the parents are deceased, names of informants and beneficiaries on death certificates and wills can give recent addresses for other family members (see Chapter 6 for information on how to find wills).

The Expatriate Community

When British people move abroad, many, understandably, wish to link with others from the UK in the country where they now live. Some countries have strong expatriate ('expat') communities. Lots of expats also like to receive news from home and link up with other Brits online.

Websites for British expats can be general or country specific. There are a number of sites that may be able to help you find a British person living abroad, through forums or advertisements:

* **http://britishexpats.com** is a general site with country-specific sections. Registration is free.
* **www.britishexpat.com** is another general site with a classified section and forums for specific countries.
* **www.british-expats.com** offers information and resources for expatriates, with free registration and various discussion forums.
* **www.contactexpats.com** is a directory of expats worldwide. Basic registration is free; the annual fee for full membership (to send emails to other members) is £6.
* **www.britsinaus.com** is a site dedicated to the British living in Australia, both permanently and temporarily.
* **www.spainexpat.com** is for all expats living in Spain, and includes free registration and forums.

There are also many **newspapers** specifically for British expats. Some contain general news from Britons anywhere in the world, such as the *Weekly Telegraph,* while others are produced in countries where there are large expat communities, for example the *Majorca Daily Bulletin* or *Tenerife News.*

Weekly Telegraph
www.telegraph.co.uk/global/index.jhtml
Telegraph Group Limited
1 Canada Square
Canary Wharf
London E14 5DT
Or use the online enquiry form on the website (click on
   'Contact us' in the lefthand index).

Majorca Daily Bulletin
www.majorcadailybulletin.es
Tel: +34 971 788 400
Email: editorial@majorcadailybulletin.es

Tenerife News
www.tenerifenews.com
Edf. Siete Fuentes
Calle Siete Fuentes, 8
38410 Los Realejos
Santa Cruz de Tenerife, España
Tel: +34 922 346 000, or 0871 8712 897 from the UK,
   or use the online enquiry form on the website

If the person you are looking for lives abroad, particularly if you know the country they live in, an expat newspaper may be the way to reach them. The publishers may be willing to print a feature if there is a 'human interest' element to the story – 'Bridesmaid sought for 50th wedding anniversary' or 'Brother needed for bone-marrow transplant', for example.

Alternatively, if a feature article is not possible, a classified advertisement in an expat newspaper may bring contact from the right person, or someone who knows them. The cost of a small advert might save you hundreds of pounds in research fees.

To find suitable newspapers, search one of the general expat websites, visit www.onlinenewspapers.com or consult *Ulrich's Periodicals Directory*, an international directory of newspapers and journals (available for reference at most main public libraries).

Radio Stations

Local and regional radio stations in other countries will often be willing to broadcast short appeals or human-interest features.

Radio Europe is a British expat station with half a million members that broadcasts to Spain, Portugal and Tenerife. The producers say that people seeking residents within their broadcast area are welcome to get in touch with their story.

You can listen on 104 FM from mainland Europe or via the internet at www.rem.fm.

Radio Europe Mediterraneo

La Colonia

REM FM Centre

San Pedro de Alcántara 29670

Marbella

Málaga

Spain

Tel: +34 952 799 953

Fax: +34 952 799 620

Another station specifically for expats is Expatsradio (www.expatsradio.com). This service is only available on the internet.

To find stations broadcasting from other countries and regions, visit one of these portal sites for links:

* www.live-radio.net/info.shtml
* www.ability.org.uk/international_radio_broadcasters.html

Property Records

If the person you are looking for owns a property in England or Wales but lives in another country, their overseas residential address should be displayed on the Land Registry title register for that property. For full details of the Land Registry (www.landreg.gov.uk) and how to obtain property ownership records, see Chapter 6.

Agencies

There are other organisations that may be able to help you with your search if it involves a missing relative.

International Social Service of the United Kingdom (ISS UK) is a charity that works together with statutory and voluntary agencies in the UK and around the world, enabling a global exchange of information and access to protection and support services for families. ISS UK aims to promote and protect the rights and welfare of children and vulnerable adults across international borders. This includes those who are separated from family members as a consequence of divorce, migration, seeking asylum, trafficking and abduction, and other vulnerable individuals for whom there are protection concerns.

> International Social Service of the United Kingdom
>   (ISS UK)
> www.issuk.org.uk
> Cranmer House
> 39 Brixton Road
> London SW9 6DD
> Tel: 020 7735 8941

Finding Grandma

Telisha was an 8-year-old Jamaican girl whose mother decided to study in the UK. After some time Telisha came to visit her mother during the school holidays. Sadly, during the visit Telisha's mother died unexpectedly and Telisha came to the attention of the local authority. Its staff were unsure what to do so contacted ISS UK for help.

ISS UK was able to contact a corresponding agency in Jamaica and, with its help, find Telisha's grandmother. Telisha is now living happily with her grandmother in Jamaica.

From www.issuk.org.uk. Reproduced with permission.

The **British Red Cross** works in countries across the world when conflict or disaster strikes. At times like these, communications often break down and families can become separated. As a result, people do not know where to turn to find missing relatives or how to get a message to them.

In these situations the British Red Cross works to restore and maintain contact by searching for missing relatives, delivering family news, tracing relatives and exchanging messages between family members. The event that has separated relatives does not have to be current; those who have lost touch in the past due to disaster or conflict may also qualify for assistance.

The website is at www.redcross.org.uk (click on 'Overseas' then 'Tracing services'). Or call the British Red Cross Head Office on 020 7877 7000 and ask for the tracing service.

Reunite is a UK charity specialising in cases of international parental child abduction. The charity provides advice, information and support to parents, family members and guardians who have had a child abducted or who fear that an abduction may be possible. It also gives advice

to parents who may have abducted their child and provides information on issues that may affect contact.

> Reunite
> www.reunite.org
> PO Box 7124
> Leicester LE1 7XX
> Tel: 0116 2556 234

The **Salvation Army** is an international organisation with
branches in numerous countries throughout the world,
and the UK headquarters of its Family Tracing Service can
be contacted for more information about finding a relative
in another country (see Chapter 8 for more details of the
Family Tracing Service).

Embassies, Consulates and High Commissions

When asked to find someone overseas, particularly if there
are no apparent UK contacts who might have their
address, I have sometimes sought advice from the British
diplomatic service in the country where the person is
thought to be living. It may take some time to receive a
response or speak to the correct person, but perseverance
can be worth it. You may be advised whether Britons in
that country require visas or if they have an obligation to
register with the embassy when living or working there. If
this is the case, the embassy may be willing to forward a
message from you. Staff may also know of public records
or agencies that can help to trace someone.

The Foreign and Commonwealth Office (FCO) has contact details of the UK's embassies, high commissions and consulates. The FCO's website is at www.fco.gov.uk (click on 'Directory' on the lefthand side, then 'UK Embassies Overseas).

Or contact Foreign and Commonwealth Office general enquiries on 020 7008 1500.

Professional Researchers

Instead of trying to learn about public records and resources in another country, commissioning a local researcher is usually the best option when looking for people overseas. The researcher will have experience with and knowledge of the records and resources available, which could save you time and money.

I have used **Cyndi's List** (www.cyndislist.com) on numerous occasions to help locate people in other countries. It was created in 1996 by genealogy enthusiast Cyndi Howells, who lives in Washington. It is one of the most popular genealogy websites in the world, with an average of more than 70,000 visitors per day. There are over 250,000 links to genealogy-related sites worldwide.

The Cyndi's List home page has a detailed index with categories, including countries, arranged alphabetically, and the site is comprehensively cross-referenced. Clicking on the country you are concerned with will lead to information about records in that country, organisations, publications and so on. The category I most often use within each country section is 'Professional Researchers, Volunteers &

Other Research Services'. This links to websites for genealogists, family researchers and organisations that have expert knowledge and access to records. Usually there are fees to pay, and a budget should be agreed before research proceeds. However, the cost is usually reasonable and the results are delivered far more quickly than they would be if you tried to carry out the research yourself.

Seeking Celia

Laura was looking for her mother, Celia, who was working as a nurse when Laura was born. Celia was ambitious and did not want to keep her baby, but her boyfriend, Warren, pleaded with her not to have the child adopted, offering to raise her himself. Celia agreed and when Laura was just a few months old Celia gained promotion and moved to a different hospital in another part of the country. When Laura was three years old, Warren married June.

'June is the only mum I have ever known. She is a nice person and I care for her deeply, but she isn't my real mum and I feel I need to meet my mother and to know her,' said Laura. 'Dad and June were a bit shocked when I told them I wanted to look for Celia. Dad, especially, was not very encouraging. He told me that my mum was not at all maternal and warned me that she might not be interested, but I still had to go ahead.'

I searched all of the usual UK records, but was unable to find Celia. However, through a genealogy website I found a member of her family and exchanged a couple of tentative messages. This revealed that Celia now lived in New Zealand with a husband and two daughters. Not knowing anything about New Zealand records, I went to Cyndi's List and found a family researcher who seemed confident that he would locate Celia and her family. He was warned that the situation was delicate and asked not to have any direct contact with anyone in the household.

Within three days the researcher, for the grand sum of £15, had found an address and phone number for Celia and her family. A couple of letters were sent without a response, so Laura took the decision to telephone. Celia answered and was at first a little hostile and cautious; her husband and daughters did not know about Laura. Realising that Laura would not just go away, Celia took her number and promised to call soon. A few days later, she phoned Laura while alone in the house and slowly, over several weeks, the two started to develop a relationship. However, Celia refused to tell her new family about Laura.

Five months after the first phone call Laura was on a plane to New Zealand to finally meet her mother. 'It all had to be a big secret,' says Laura, 'and to this day my mother's family, including my half-sisters, don't know about me, which makes me rather sad.' The trip was nevertheless a success, with Celia using a spa break as an excuse to meet her daughter. Laura said, 'I hope that one day Celia will tell her family and that I will get to meet them, but in the meantime I'm very happy with what we have.'

The **Association of Professional Genealogists** (APG) was founded in the US in 1979 as a not-for-profit organisation, with the aim of focusing the efforts of professional genealogists and researchers worldwide and supporting them in all areas of their work. There are now more than 1,600 members from all over the world who offer a range of assistance, including genealogy, living family research and probate services. Members should be competent and experienced. Although there is no formal application procedure that requires proof of ability, applications for membership are checked by the association and members must agree to follow the APG's code of practice.

The APG has an online directory of members, which can be searched by name, geographical area or specialist subject. Although the organisation is based in the US, there a high number of members in other countries too. On the APG's website (www.apgen.org), click on 'How to Find a Professional', select or enter your search terms, and you will be presented with a list of researchers who fulfil your criteria. Each entry on the list hyperlinks to more information about the researcher and their contact details.

Association of Professional Genealogists
www.apgen.org
P.O. Box 350998
Westminster
Colorado CO 80035-0998
USA

Family History Societies

In Chapter 4 we looked at the Federation of Family History Societies (FFHS) and how to find a local society through its website. The Federation also has links with a number of societies in Australia, Canada, New Zealand and the US.

Visiting www.ffhs.org.uk/General/Members/Overseas.htm will take you to the overseas societies section of the website, where you will find a list of family history societies for each country. The associations shown are not only general but also specific to particular cities, states and regions. The policy may vary on publishing appeals for information about relatives, and some societies may ask that you pay a subscription before they will consider this, but fees are nominal and if you're successful the investment may save you much more.

Country-Specific Resources

Countries where large numbers of Britons have gone to live, whether in the distant or recent past, will always retain connections with the UK. Consequently I have conducted research on many occasions in particular areas and have become familiar with some of the records and resources available.

The **United States of America** has a Freedom of Information Act that, in most cases, makes family research much easier than in other countries. Although some public records are state based and are not available online, personal details about a high percentage of US nationals can be accessed on the internet.

USSearch (www.ussearch.com) maintains a vast network of databases containing information from sources such as public records, phone books and marketing lists.

From the home page, enter a surname, first name and approximate age. The database searches millions of records and display a list of preliminary results – name, age and state of residence. If there is an entry that you think may be correct, click on the name and complete the application. At this stage you need to enter your credit card details; fees range from around $10 to $100 for an expert-assisted comprehensive 'People Locate' search, depending on how much information you require. Results will be available to view instantly and will also be emailed to you.

Intellius (www.intellius.com) is similar to USSearch in terms of the records searched and the information provided, but the search form on the home page requires just a forename and surname. Preliminary results also show other family members within the household. Where telephone numbers, dates of birth and postal addresses will be available with your report, this is indicated on the preliminary results page. After creating an account and registering your credit card details, select a name to discover how many records have been found about the person and the cost of each report; costs range from under $10 to around $50 for a full background check.

The **Social Security Death Index** (SSDI; http://ssdi.rootsweb.com) is one of the largest and easiest-to-use databases for US genealogical and family research. It holds millions of death records that date from 1937. In 1962 records were computerised and became more complete. The SSDI is not entirely comprehensive, however, and cannot be compared with death indexes in the UK.

Enter a surname, first name and middle name or initial into the search boxes for a list of results. If the name you are searching on is common there is also an advanced search option. You will be presented with a list of matches giving dates of birth and death, place of last residence and social security number. There are options for ordering a death certificate and also a pre-printed letter to assist you if you would like to apply for a copy of the deceased's social security application form (at a cost of $27). The death certificate will give place of birth, maiden name if appropriate, and name of the informant/next of kin.

Policy does vary from state to state regarding the issue of death certificates. Some can be ordered online without a problem, but some states ask for the applicant's own social security details and limit access to relatives of the deceased. If there is any problem with ordering a death certificate online, you may find it helpful to engage a US researcher to complete the application for you. Go to www.apgen.org to choose a researcher in the correct state.

Australia has fairly strict data protection laws, with restrictions on access to birth, marriage and death records. Electoral registers used to be public, although they were never published online, but recent privacy laws mean that most current registers are no longer available. Some states do allow access to recent and historical registers, although they are usually in microfiche format and only searchable by personal visit to the library where they are held.

Local researchers may be commissioned to search **electoral registers and directories** for you. To find a researcher, visit the AAGRA website:

Association of Australian Genealogists and Record
  Agents
www.aagra.asn.au
PO Box 268 Oakleigh
Victoria 3166
Australia

The **online telephone directories** for Australia can only be searched by individual state, not for the whole country simultaneously. White Pages results also display the postal address and often the initials of both main residents where a couple lives in the same household. The website for White Pages Online is www.whitepages.com.au.

Lots of letters

Clare and her sister Penny knew that they had a cousin in Australia, but didn't know how to contact him. Their father had a younger sister called Rosemary who went to live near Melbourne in the 1960s, married there and had a son called Gerald.

Clare and Penny's father died almost 20 years ago and his second wife kept all of his belongings, including family photographs and letters. They fell out with her over this and had no way of finding out any more about this cousin they had never met. They were not even sure of his surname, although they thought it was Sanders or Saunders.

One Sunday while Clare was playing with her first computer, she started looking for any online resources that might help them to find Gerald. The Australian White Pages came up and she entered 'G Sanders' then 'G Saunders' on the search page, selecting Victoria, the state where Melbourne is located. She called Penny over to see what she thought and they started printing off the pages of results. They were rather daunted as they had over 60 possible addresses and no way of knowing if any of them could relate to their cousin.

Over the next few weeks they drafted a chatty letter, photocopied some family information and pictures onto a sheet, then bought some labels, envelopes and stamps. They decided to send out the letters in batches of six, waiting about a month before sending out the next ones, allowing time for the return post. When they sent the first lot of letters they were very excited, but after the first three batches brought no response they started to feel disheartened and almost gave up.

More than six months later, three weeks after sending out batch number five, Clare got a letter from Australia through the letterbox. It was quite thick, in a large white envelope and had several stamps on it. She knew straight away that it was from Gerald. She called Penny and they decided to meet up so they could open the letter together.

Later that afternoon, in their favourite coffee shop, they could hardly contain their excitement as they opened the letter and took in all of its contents. It was wonderful. There was a warm and friendly letter from Gerald, photographs of him and his family, and some interesting documents relating to Clare and Penny's father's ancestry. Gerald had been attempting to research his family tree from a distance over the past few years, gathering lots of information about grandparents and great-grandparents. The women were amazed and very impressed, as there was an awful lot that they didn't know. What was most touching was that he also sent them an invitation to his daughter's wedding later that year.

After taking in all that Gerald had sent them, they went back to Penny's house, checked the time difference and called their cousin for what turned out to be a very long conversation. He was very pleased to hear from them and each woman spent more than half an hour talking to him. Unfortunately they couldn't make it to the wedding, but they have all remained in regular contact through phone calls, emails and letters. Gerald is hoping to visit the UK within the next year and Clare and Penny are saving up for an extended trip to Australia in two years' time. They think themselves so lucky to have found such a lovely cousin and it was well worth the time they invested sending all those letters.

As in the UK, there is a national organisation in Australia for missing and vulnerable people. The **National Missing Persons Coordination Centre** can offer help where there is concern for the safety or wellbeing of a person who has not been in contact.

Missing Persons Coordination Centre
http://afp.gov.au/national/missing/nmpcc
PO Box 401
Canberra City ACT 2601
Australia

Canada also has strict data protection legislation relating to personal information, including birth, marriage and death records. Records relating to births less than 100 years ago, marriages less than 80 years ago and deaths less than 70 years ago are strictly confidential. To apply for historical records that may contain useful family information, you need to contact the civil registration agency for the province or territory concerned. For a helpful summary of contact details, go to http://globalgenealogy.com/global gazette/gazfd/gazfd71a.htm, an article in *The Global Gazette*, Canada's online family history magazine.

Canada411 is the country's White and Yellow Pages, and has online searchable directory services at www.canada411.ca. Results also display the postal address.

As in the UK, obituaries can be used as a resource for tracing living people. In addition to details about the deceased, you can often find information about other family members and where they live. The **Ottawa Citizen** (www.ottawacitizen.com) has an online, searchable obituary index (select 'Obituaries at Remembering' from the lefthand list then scroll to the bottom of the page and click on 'Local resources').

You may also want to consult burial records. The **Ontario Cemetery Finding Aid** (www.islandnet.com/ocfa) is a searchable database of over two million interments in the state, together with information about how to apply for full records from the appropriate authorities. Or try www.interment.net, a free online library of burial records from thousands of cemeteries across the world.

Chapter Ten

CONTACTING PEOPLE YOU FIND

When your search is over and you at last have contact details for the person you are seeking, what happens next? You may be tempted to jump in the car, get on a train, take a bus and just turn up. Why not surprise them? They are sure to be pleased to see you.

If the 'surprise' approach is the first that springs to mind, please do resist, or at least consider it carefully. Turning up at the home of someone you may not have seen for a number of years may make them feel uneasy or even threatened. They may be resentful at your unexpected arrival, particularly as they will be unprepared and perhaps not at their best.

You should also consider carefully whether making a phone call out of the blue to the person you have been seeking is a good idea. They may be having a difficult time, be very busy or stressed. Putting them on the spot with an unexpected phone call may not be the best way to make your approach.

I prefer writing a letter in the first instance, and always recommend this approach to others. A short note with a choice of return contact details is probably the best option. Always include a 'get-out clause' for the recipient so that you know the letter was actually delivered. Something like this usually works well:

> *If you do not wish to have contact at this time, for whatever reason, I will respect this. All I ask is that you drop me a short note or email just to confirm that you have received my letter, and I won't bother you again. Do contact me at any time in the future if you change your mind.*

If you are not 100 per cent sure that the address you have is correct or up to date, enclose a covering note and a stamped addressed envelope and ask the recipient to let you know if the details are wrong or the person you are seeking has moved.

What If You Get No Response?

If you don't receive an answer to your letter, there may be a number of reasons. For example:

* The person might be on holiday or away.
* They may be busy and haven't got around to replying.
* They may be going through a difficult time.
* They might be thinking about whether they wish to renew the relationship.
* They might not have received the letter.
* The letter may have been intercepted by someone else in the household.
* They may be intending to respond but waiting for the right time.
* They may have moved very recently but still be shown as resident on the records that you checked.

* They may not want contact so have decided to ignore your letter.

Although a lack of response may lead you to conclude that contact is not welcome, there are several possibilities, so don't give up if you don't hear anything. I usually suggest waiting at least three weeks before considering following up on an unanswered letter. After this you could write another short note with a copy of the original or, if you have a telephone number, try calling just to ask whether your letter was received.

To illustrate that there is a range of potential outcomes, here are two similar stories with very different results.

Big brother in England

Cliff says that the day he spoke to his father again after 29 years was the best day of his life.

Cliff's mother and father had divorced when Cliff was five. His father, Richard, was in the navy and away at sea regularly. 'I have vague memories of a large man in uniform with sandy hair carrying me,' said Cliff, 'a few photographs of my parents when they got married and just one picture of me as a baby sitting on my dad's knee.' Cliff is a successful software designer and, after four years of marriage and two lovely children, he decided that he would very much like to see his father again.

Cliff's mother was helpful and told him everything she could remember about Richard and his family. He had been an only child and his parents, Harold and Margaret Newman, lived in Peterborough. Cliff searched internet directories for his father, but there were too many people with the same name. He looked for his grandparents, but did not find any entries for a couple with those names in or near Peterborough. He did find a Margaret Newman listed who appeared to live alone, so he printed off the address and kept it in his wallet.

Several months later a business trip led him near Peterborough and this prompted him to pay a visit to Margaret Newman's address. Cliff found a young-looking 70 year old weeding her front garden. He asked if she was Mrs Newman and she started to reply but, looking up at him, she suddenly exclaimed, 'I know who you are!' She was indeed his grandmother and was overjoyed to see him. She invited him in, hugged him, cried and told Cliff how she had thought about and missed him over the years.

'I could not have had a warmer welcome,' said Cliff, 'and it was really quite emotional.' He was surprised to see a picture of himself as a toddler on a shelf in Margaret's living room. Over a cup of tea, she related how Richard had settled in New Zealand after leaving the navy 12 years earlier. Margaret had nagged him to keep in touch with Cliff and Richard had always intended to, but he was busy with a second wife and twin sons, now aged 14. Margaret promised to call Richard and let him know that Cliff had made contact, so Cliff left feeling very happy.

When he arrived home from work the next day, his wife said that his father had called and wanted to hear from him. Cliff nervously dialled the number, Richard answered and they had a long, easy conversation. Richard's wife, Julie, had known about Cliff all along and the twins had been told about their 'big brother in England'.

Richard had always intended to find Cliff and was planning a trip to England the following year. The two share an interest in computers and now keep in touch by email, exchanging news and family photographs.

Ten months after Cliff first called on his grandmother, he, Margaret and Richard sat together in the same room and talked for hours while their families got to know each other. Cliff gets along well with his half-brothers and feels very close to his dad. 'It was very hard to say goodbye to them all, especially my dad,' said Cliff, 'but we are planning to visit them in a couple of years. In the meantime there is always email and very big phone bills! Things just couldn't be better.'

'Forget it'

Julia had never got along well with her mother, Sandra, and it didn't help that she was never told about her father. Sandra described him as a 'one-night stand' and Julia only knew that his name was Ron. This information had come from her aunt Jean, as her mother refused to discuss their relationship or tell Julia anything about him. 'It was very frustrating,' said Julia, 'because every time I mentioned anything or tried to approach the subject, my mum would either clam up or walk out.'

Working as an air hostess meant that Julia had little time for research and she did not yet feel ready to buy a home of her own, being away so often. She moved in with her aunt as a temporary measure, but the arrangement worked well for both of them and she stayed.

After her mother's death, Julia decided that it was time to look for her dad. She grilled Jean for more information. She found out that far from her father being a one-night stand her parents had lived together for almost a year, but Ron was already married to someone else. When he discovered that Sandra was pregnant, he returned to his wife. Julia's birth certificate did not show a father's name but Jean remembered that his surname was Bignell.

A search of marriage records showed a Ronald Bignell getting married in the right area eight years before Julia was born. She applied for the certificate and Ronald's occupation was recorded as 'surveyor', which matched what Jean remembered. Armed with this information, Julia went to the local library and looked at the directory for surveyors. It was a little out of date, but it showed a Ronald Bignell listed as working not far from where he had lived with Julia's mother. 'I decided to be brave and call his office,' said Julia, 'but they told me that he had retired almost two years ago, which was a bit of a blow.' An online electoral register search than found Ronald and his wife Susan living nearby.

Julia spent many hours composing a letter to her father. It was thoughtful and well considered, assuring him that she wanted nothing more than to meet him once and ask him a few questions. She requested that he contact her, then waited. After two weeks she went off on a four-day trip to New York.

While she was away, her father called Jean and asked, 'What does she want?' Jean tried to explain that, as Sandra had died, Julia really just wanted to know a little about her father. Ronald replied briskly, 'Her letter could have caused a lot of trouble.' Jean gathered from this that Ron's wife did not wish to be reminded of her husband's infidelity. Ron asked Jean to tell Julia to 'forget it'.

Julia was obviously upset when she returned to this news and at first felt like going round to her father's house to confront him. However, she realised that this would be counterproductive. 'I try hard to remain optimistic,' she said, 'and hope that he will eventually change his mind. In the meantime, I'll just keep busy with my work, but I still feel that something is missing from my life.'

Using an Intermediary

If your contact with the person you are seeking is likely to cause some shock, upset or disruption, please consider using an intermediary to make the first approach. This is particularly relevant when seeking a natural parent. An intermediary is someone who may be slightly more detached from the situation and who is trustworthy and mature enough not to sabotage the chances of a reunion. The following could be considered suitable intermediaries:

* Relative (who may be known to both parties)
* Social worker
* Counsellor
* Family doctor
* Vicar
* Researcher
* Mutual friend

At least I tried

Mark and Carole had grown up together and attended the same schools. When they were 17 they got engaged and thought they would spend the rest of their lives together. When Carole started making wedding plans soon after her 18th birthday, Mark got an acute, severe attack of cold feet. While for a few months he went along with Carole's plans, when she became pregnant the weight of predictability and responsibility was too much for such a young man. Nicole was born and he adored her, but even this could not make him stay.

Mark made hasty plans, leaving Carole, her parents and his family distraught when he left with a friend for America to find work. He never came back to England to live and although he did attempt to see Nicole once when she was about 3 years old, he was turned away by her angry grandmother, who told him that Carole was married and her new husband was much better than him!

Mark married, had four children and built a successful business in America, but he never forgot Nicole. When his youngest daughter graduated, he was starting to think about early retirement and, along with their plans for a new way of life, he and his wife arranged to make their wills. Mark decided immediately that Nicole should be included as a beneficiary – he dug out her birth certificate and baby pictures and became very emotional. He wanted so much to find her, tell her he was sorry for leaving her and attempt to build some kind of relationship, but feared that he was way too late. He discovered through family contacts living locally that Nicole had taken the surname of her stepfather when he married her mother, and there was a possibility that she did not even know that her mother's husband was not her biological father.

Mark thought long and hard about what to do. He talked to his wife, his mother and his sister. In the end he decided that he could not live with himself if he did not try to make contact with Nicole: she needed to be found so that at the very least her current details could be entered in his will. Nicole was indeed located, married and living not far from her mother. Her marriage certificate recorded her step-father, not Mark, as her father.

Now that he had her current name and address, Mark agonised for days over whether to make contact but, having come this far, decided that he could not leave things. He spent hours drafting and redrafting a loving and emotional let-ter to Nicole and eventually sent it to her, enclosing lots of family photographs. He said that he hoped his approach was not a shock to her, he apologised for leaving her mother and not keeping in contact, and he asked her to get in touch to talk about the possibility of their getting to know one another. Not wanting to risk the letter being opened by someone else and preferring to use a personal approach, Mark hired a female investigator, who seemed sensitive and capable, in the area where Nicole lived to deliver the letter by hand.

When the investigator approached Nicole and tried to give her the letter, Nicole became very hostile. She knew about Mark but had been told lots of negative things about him by her family. She grabbed the letter and wrote 'I don't want to know you – please do not contact me again' on it and gave it back to the investigator with threats to contact the police if she heard from her father again.

Fortunately, the investigator managed to calm Nicole down, take her for a coffee and persuade her to read the letter properly. By the end of the meeting Nicole had agreed to send her father a letter and a photograph.

The letter Mark received was brief, just saying that Nicole did not feel able to see him or continue to communicate. She wished him well, but said that too many years had gone by. She had a great relationship with her mum and stepfather, which she did not want to spoil.

'At least I know for sure that Nicole received my letter and photographs and I'm not left wondering what she really thinks,' says Mark. 'I treasure her letter and picture. If I could turn back the clock I would do things differently. Of course the outcome is not as I wanted, but I'm relatively content that at least I tried. I just hope that, one day, Nicole will change her mind and get in touch.'

Respect the Response

If the response is not as you expected or hoped, it can be counterproductive to pursue or try to persuade the other person to think differently. You will not know all their circumstances, and it is possible that they may have a change of heart in the future. Just be sure that you send all of your contact details, and stress that you will be happy to hear from them at any time.

Do also remember that there are laws against harassment, stalking and causing nuisance. Be patient and you might be rewarded.

Getting to Know Each Other

When you do find a long-lost relative or friend and the response is positive, there is often a 'honeymoon' period when the relationship is a novelty. It can be tempting to call one another constantly and want to visit as often as possible, particularly with new-found relatives or people you haven't seen for many years. But taking things slowly is usually the best way: get to know each other or rediscover your relationship gradually and it will be more likely to endure.

Start by exchanging letters or emails, progress to phone conversations if you're both in agreement, and when you're ready you can arrange to meet up for a chat. It is probably best to meet on neutral territory first unless there are specific reasons not to, such as lack of transport or limited mobility. Make arrangements to meet in a public place such as a park or a café. Having a set time that you need to leave makes things less awkward if you do run out of things to talk about. Take things along with you that are relevant, for example family photographs, documents, charts, letters or other items that are likely to be of interest.

If after this you arrange to visit one another, make the date some weeks in the future, then if this goes well, perhaps a return visit at least a few weeks after that. Emails, letters and phone calls can maintain the contact between meetings, but make sure that the effort is not one-sided. If you begin to sense that the other person isn't quite so keen or they start to ignore your messages, it may be an idea to cool things down and wait for them to contact you again first. After several months, you may naturally settle into a routine with regular or occasional contact and visits.

Like being in love

Caroline, Wayne's wife, called me to ask if I could help find her husband's sister. Wayne had not seen his younger sister Mandy since they had been sent to separate foster homes as teenagers. They had grown up together in care since their mother, a single parent, had died when Wayne was just 4 years old; Mandy was only 2 at the time. They were close as children but less so as teenagers. 'We had different things in common at the time and different friends, of course. Calling or writing to your little sister doesn't seem that important when you're 15,' said Wayne.

After college, Wayne got a job and became absorbed in his work and social life. He had lots of friends and through one of them he met Caroline. 'I wanted to ask Mandy to the wedding,' he said, 'and did try to contact her, but she had moved.'

I located Mandy and put the two of them in touch with each other. Their first phone call went on for over an hour – there was so much to talk about. Calls soon became a daily event and then Mandy also started to visit. She would some-times stay until very late and talk with Wayne constantly. 'It was a bit like being in love,' said Wayne. 'I wanted to see her as often as possible and missed her if she wasn't around. I wanted to hug her all the time, scared that she would disappear again.'

Caroline started to feel excluded and resentful of their relationship, which caused tension within the marriage.

Matters became worse when Wayne suggested that Mandy come on holiday with them. Caroline flipped, packed a bag and left to stay with her mother, telling Wayne that he could call her in a week. Despite Wayne's efforts, she refused any contact, sending him just one note asking him to consider how much their marriage meant to him and to question the nature of his relationship with his sister.

'That week was the longest of my life,' said Wayne, 'and very sobering. I thought how I would feel if Caroline had a relationship like mine and Mandy's and realised that I would be very jealous. Also, I thought about Mandy and realised that she wasn't going to go anywhere. Now that we were in touch again we could have a normal brother and sister relationship without upsetting my wife.'

After hours of talking and compromising, Caroline and Wayne agreed some rules and boundaries relating to Mandy: Caroline would make an effort to be welcoming and friendly, while Wayne would cool things down, see Mandy less often and limit his previously numerous phone conversations with his sister. 'It took almost a year for things to really settle down,' said Caroline, 'and for us both to become comfortable with the arrangements, but things are about right now. Mandy and Wayne speak every few days on the phone and she visits us every couple of weeks. I feel now as though we have our normal life back.'

With hindsight, Wayne now wishes that he had taken matters more slowly in the first place.

DNA Tests

Sometimes the circumstances of a reunion are such that there is some uncertainty about the genetic connection between the two parties.

One obvious example is where there might be a question of **paternity**. If a natural father is found who did not know about his child or has doubts whether he is the father, a DNA test can confirm or rule out his paternity.

The procedure for determining paternity is a very simple saliva swab. However, there can be huge emotional consequences and the decision to test should not be taken lightly. You might also need counselling before undertaking a DNA test, to consider if the decision to do so is correct or how you might feel if the results are not as you hope. A surprise result can be devastating.

Results for paternity tests can prove 100 per cent if there is no biological connection between an alleged father and child. A positive result can be 99.99 per cent accurate in proving the probability that the alleged father is the parent of the child.

The UK government issued a code of practice in 2001 for paternity testing services. Companies should now be accredited by the Department for Constitutional Affairs (DCA). A list of approved laboratories can be obtained from the DCA:

Department for Constitutional Affairs
www.dca.gov.uk/family/paternity.htm
Family Relationships Branch 2

Family Justice Division
4th Floor, Selborne House
54–60 Victoria Street
London SW1E 6QW
Tel: 020 7210 2653
Fax: 020 7210 8681
Email: paternity.enquiries@hmcourts-service.gsi.gov.uk

Tests can also be undertaken to determine whether two or more persons share a **common ancestor**; that is, whether their genetic relationship is sibling (brother or sister), cousin, grandparent–grandchild or uncle/aunt–nephew/niece.

These tests can be used for private curiosity, family research, inheritance claims, immigration rights and degrees of kinship. As with paternity tests, kinship DNA tests should not be undertaken lightly. The results from this type of test are not as accurate as paternity tests, but can still establish a high degree of probability, depending on the nature of the genetic relationship and the number of relatives available for testing.

Many of the companies approved for paternity testing also carry out tests for sibling and other relationships.

Important note: the Human Tissue Act 2004 created a new offence of DNA theft. It is now illegal to obtain and test a person's DNA without their consent.

Keeping in Touch

Unfortunately, relatives and friends are sometimes reunited only to lose touch again due to mutual neglect or apathy. Also, if one party is always the first one to make contact, they can become disheartened if the other doesn't take the initiative on some occasions.

So when contact has been established and family or friends have eventually been reunited, how can you ensure that the relationship continues?

The **telephone** is an obvious way to keep in touch and up to date with each other's news, but calls can be expensive. Advances with internet phones and software such as Skype can reduce the cost significantly, even for international calls.

Email has made communication cheap, easy and quick. Messages can come across as impersonal, however. It is a good way to stay in touch for those who may be lazy or short of time but, in my opinion, emails are no substitute for meetings or proper conversation.

Phone and email can also be unsuitable for maintaining contact between a group of relatives or friends. They can only be used to communicate between two people at once, unless conference calls can be arranged or if emails are copied to all parties.

The internet has some useful **sites** that help families and groups to stay in touch. For example, My Family (www.myfamily.com) creates a personal family or group site with a secure log-in for each member. Within the private space, there are facilities to exchange news and messages, enter anniversary and birthday details and upload photographs. Keeping up to date in this way is also cost effective when compared with phone, post and travel expenses. My Family usually offers a free trial period, with a current annual subscription of $29.95 for 1GB of storage.

Letters written by hand and sent through the mail are becoming less popular since the internet became the preferred way for people to communicate. However, a handwritten envelope containing a personal letter and perhaps some photographs or family documents can make the usual postal delivery of bills and junk mail much more exciting. Post is still relatively cheap and the tangible pages and enclosures can be kept for future generations.

There is no substitute, however, for **meeting up** with people, even once every year or two. You can truly connect by seeing each other face to face, shaking hands, exchanging hugs and engaging in close conversation.

Plan meetings, gatherings and reunions well in advance, preferably earmarking a date each time for the next one. Consider travel arrangements, accommodation if necessary, access for the disabled if required and food preferences. It is best to work out in advance how the gathering will be paid for. Will each person or couple pay for their own accommodation and food, for example, or will someone be in charge of collecting funds and paying the bills?

Having invested the time and trouble to find someone from your past, it is worth making an effort, using a combination of the above methods, to create an enduring relationship.

FURTHER READING

The Primal Wound: Understanding the Adopted Child, Nancy Verrier (Nancy Verrier, 1993, ISBN 9780963648006)

Adoption Reunion Handbook, Liz Trinder, Julia Feast and David Howe (John Wiley, 2004, ISBN 9780470094228)

Family Reunion Planning Kit for Dummies, Cheryl Fall (Hungry Minds, 2001, ISBN 9780764553998)

Hello Dad: Finding Your Father and Getting to Know Him, Karen Bali (Writers Printshop, 2004, ISBN 9781904623106)

DNA and Family History, Chris Pomery (The National Archives, 2004, ISBN 9781903365700)

Track Down Your Ancestors: Draw Up Your Family Tree, Estelle Catlett (Elliot Right Way Books, 2003, ISBN 9780716021513)

Tracing Your Scottish Ancestors: The Official Guide, Scottish Record Office (Mercat Press, 2003, ISBN 9781841830599)

After Pomp and Circumstance: High School Reunion as an Autobiographical Occasion, Vered Vinitzky-Serous (University of Chicago Press, 1998, ISBN 9780226856698)

ACKNOWLEDGEMENTS

This book is dedicated to my wonderful husband Sunil, my super children, Sitara and Ashwin, and also my mum, Ann.

Special thanks to Frances for proofreading, Fleur for her encouragement, my agent, Liz, and my friends for their support: Barbara, Heather, David, Sharon, Sally and Jane.

INDEX